CliffsNotes™

Beowulf

By Stanley P. Baldwin, M.A.

IN THIS BOOK

- Learn about the Beowulf Poet
- Preview an Introduction to the Poem
- Explore themes, literary devices, and recurring images in the Critical Commentaries
- Examine in-depth Character Analyses
- Acquire an understanding of the epic with Critical Essays
- Reinforce what you learn with CliffsNotes Review
- Find additional information to further your study in CliffsNotes Resource Center and online at www.cliffsnotes.com

Wiley Publishing, Inc.

About the Author
Stanley P. Baldwin is a writer and teacher in Nebraska.

Publisher's Acknowledgments
Editorial
Project Editor: Tracy Barr
Acquisitions Editor: Greg Tubach
Glossary Editors: The editors and staff of Webster's New World Dictionaries
Reprint Editor: Michelle Hacker
Production
Indexer: York Production Services, Inc.
Proofreader: York Production Services, Inc.

Wiley Publishing, Inc., Indianapolis Composition Services

CliffsNotes™ *Beowulf*

Published by:
Wiley Publishing, Inc.
111 River Street
Hoboken, NJ 07030
www.wiley.com

Copyright © 2000 Wiley Publishing, Inc., New York, New York
ISBN: 0-7645-8580-8

Printed in the United States of America

10 9 8 7 6 5

1O/RQ/RQ/QS/IN

Published by Wiley Publishing, Inc., New York, NY
Published simultaneously in Canada

Library of Congress Cataloging-in-Publication Data
Baldwin, Stanley.
CliffsNotes Beowulf / by Stanley Baldwin.
p. cm.
Includes bibliographical references.
ISBN 0-7645-8580-0 (alk. paper)
1. Beowulf--Examinations--Study guides. 2 Epic poetry, English (Old)--Examinations--Studyguides. 3. Heroes in literature. 4. Monsters in literature. I. Title: Beowulf. II. Title.
PR1585v .B24 2000
821'.1--dc21   00--036954
                                    CIP

No part of this publication may be reproduced, stored in a retrieval system, or transmitted in any form or by any means, electronic, mechanical, photocopying, recording, scanning, or otherwise, except as permitted under Sections 107 or 108 of the 1976 United States Copyright Act, without either the prior written permission of the Publisher, or authorization through payment of the appropriate per-copy fee to the Copyright Clearance Center, 222 Rosewood Drive, Danvers, MA 01923, 978-750-8400, fax 978-750-4744. Requests to the Publisher for permission should be addressed to the Legal Department, Wiley Publishing, Inc., 10475 Crosspoint Blvd., Indianapolis, IN 46256, 317-572-3447, fax 317-572-4447, or e-mail permcoordinator@wiley.com

For general information on our other products and services or to obtain technical support, please contact our Customer Care Department within the U.S. at 800-762-2974, outside the U.S. at 317-572-3993, or fax 317-572-4002.

Wiley also publishes its books in a variety of electronic formats. Some content that appears in print may not be available in electronic books.

Table of Contents

How to Use This Book

This CliffsNotes study guide on Beowulf supplements the original literary work, giving you background information about the author, an introduction to the work, a graphical character map, critical commentaries, expanded glossaries, and a comprehensive index, all for you to use as an educational tool that will allow you to better understand Beowulf. This study guide was written with the assumption that you have read Beowulf. Reading a literary work doesn't mean that you immediately grasp the major themes and devices used by the author; this study guide will help supplement your reading to be sure you get all you can from Beowulf. CliffsNotes Review tests your comprehension of the original text and reinforces learning with questions and answers, practice projects, and more. For further information on Beowulf, check out the CliffsNotes Resource Center.

CliffsNotes provides the following icons to highlight essential elements of particular interest:

 Reveals the underlying themes in the work.

 Helps you to more easily relate to or discover the depth of a character.

 Uncovers elements such as setting, atmosphere, mystery, passion, violence, irony, symbolism, tragedy, foreshadowing, and satire.

 Enables you to appreciate the nuances of words and phrases.

Don't Miss Our Web Site

Discover classic literature as well as modern-day treasures by visiting the CliffsNotes Web site at www.cliffsnotes.com. You can obtain a quick download of a CliffsNotes title, purchase a title in print form, browse our catalog, or view online samples.

You'll also find interactive tools that are fun and informative, links to interesting Web sites, tips, articles, and additional resources to help you, not only for literature, but for test prep, finance, careers, computers, and the Internet too. See you at www.cliffsnotes.com!

LIFE AND BACKGROUND OF THE POET

The following abbreviated biography is provided so that you might become more familiar with the historical times that possibly influenced this writing. Read this Life and Background of the Poet section and recall it when reading Beowulf, thinking of any thematic relationship between the poet's work and his life.

The Beowulf Poet

In modern, written poetry, we often judge the excellence of the creator by the use of unusual but appropriate imagery. The more original the poem is, the better. The bards who performed in the oral-formulaic tradition, however, were evaluated for the skill with which they could weave together *familiar* phrases in that poetic tradition in order to tell a story that was either already known to the audience or that was an extemporaneous effort by the *scop* (a traveling bard).

The poet's apprenticeship would have included learning certain traditional themes, popular stories, names of various characters, *and* the formulas through which the bard eventually performed the tales or created his own stories. We might expect a performer to be able to fit the theme of the piece, and even the length, to a particular occasion, as Hrothgar's *scop* does in *Beowulf.* The more accomplished bard would be the one who made most effective use of the common arsenal of formulas. A popular piece might be presented over the course of two or three or more evenings.

If a poet happened upon an especially effective formula of his own, the phrasing would become part of the oral-formulaic lexicon. Borrowing images or phrases from each other was accepted and expected. Francis P. Magoun, Jr., a noted Beowulf scholar, closely examined the first 50 verses of *Beowulf* and found that approximately 70 percent appear entirely or in part in other Anglo-Saxon poetry, even though there were only about 30,000 lines of Old English poems available for comparison. Magoun maintains that virtually all of the phrasing could be found elsewhere if we had a larger body of Anglo-Saxon works.

This clearly alters how we look at the "authorship" of the poem. Some scholars suggest that the person who put together the extant version of *Beowulf* was no more than an editor or organizer of poems created by others, probably over generations. Others credit the poet with considerable creativity while welcoming the evidence of oral tradition. It may be that a trained *scop* dictated the work to a scribe or that the poet had become literate, probably educated at one of the monasteries that existed in England at the time, which could account for the Christian influences in what probably was originally a pagan poem. Whatever the method was, the excellence of the work implies that the final result was the product of *one* very talented poet.

The Manuscript

We cannot be certain when the Anglo-Saxon poem *Beowulf* was composed, how it was created, or exactly when it was written down. What we can do is pay attention to top scholars in the field and make some pretty good guesses.

The only surviving manuscript of *Beowulf* is written in Old English (Anglo-Saxon). Rather than being composed at a specific time, the poem probably developed out of various influences, especially folk tales and traditions. Parts of it may have originally been performed by court poets or traveling bards (*scops*, pronounced "shops," in the Anglo-Saxon) who would have sung or chanted their poems to the accompaniment of a musical instrument such as a harp. We can conclude, then, that the work grew out of popular art forms, that various influences worked together, and that the story may have changed as it developed.

During the late 1920s and early 1930s, an American scholar named Milman Parry revolutionized the study of live performances of epics. He demonstrated convincingly that ancient Greek poems (the *Iliad* and the *Odyssey*) were composed in an oral-formulaic style based on tradition and designed to help the performer produce a long piece from memory *or* improvise material as he went along.

Francis P. Magoun, Jr., in his essay, "The Oral-Formulaic Character of Anglo-Saxon Narrative Poetry," published in the literary journal *Speculum* in 1953 (Vol. XXVIII, 446–467), demonstrates that the poems were recited or, more likely, sung or chanted, to audiences in the way that similar works are presented in *Beowulf*. An example in the epic itself is the performance of *The Finnsburh Episode* (lines 1063 ff.) when Hrothgar's *scop* honors Beowulf for his victory over Grendel. Magoun points out that the bards relied on language specifically developed for the poetry, formulas worked out over a long period of time and designed to fit the metrical demands of a given line while expressing whatever ideas the poet wished to communicate.

Although primarily a pagan poem, *Beowulf* contains Christian allusions that cannot be ignored. There is no mention of Jesus in *Beowulf*, and references to God seem based on the Old Testament rather than the New. But King Hrothgar and Beowulf sometimes refer to a single, all-powerful God, and there are instances of symbolic rebirth in the poem, such as Beowulf's emergence from the mere after his defeat of Grendel's mother. The fight with the dragon, late in the poem, especially seems to have Christian overtones. Counting the thief, Beowulf is accompanied by 12 associates, most of whom desert him (reminding us of Christ's apostles). We are told that God's will is done throughout the poem.

Still, many of the Christian references have the feel of afterthoughts. It seems more likely that they were added to the work as it developed—not necessarily by one *scop* or scribe but by several, all trying to make the poem more palatable to an increasingly Christian audience. The manuscript that we end up with is clearly influenced by Christian philosophy but remains heavily heroic.

What, then, can we conclude about the making of *Beowulf*? The poem was created in the oral-formulaic mode, based on folk tales and tradition, and probably composed as a whole sometime in the eighth century (700–800 AD) in England. The setting of the action *in the epic* is Denmark and Sweden in the fifth or sixth centuries, but the tone probably was altered to appeal to later audiences. Although a number of *scops* may have contributed to the poem's development, our version most likely was the creation of one poet. While the poem may have been altered over the 200 or more years before it was set down in writing, the oral-formulaic tradition would have limited the changes. It was written late in the tenth century (circa 1000 AD) by a scribe who probably was educated in a Christian monastery. He may have been a *scop* himself, or the work could have been dictated to him.

Beowulf may or may not be the first great heroic poem in English literature, as some scholars claim. It is, however, the one that survived.

INTRODUCTION TO *BEOWULF*

The following Introduction section is provided solely as an educational tool and is not meant to replace the experience of your reading the novel. Read the Introduction and A Brief Synopsis to enhance your understanding of the novel and to prepare yourself for the critical thinking that should take place whenever you read any work of fiction or nonfiction. Keep the List of Characters and Character Map at hand so that as you read the original literary work, if you encounter a character about whom you're uncertain, you can refer to the List of Characters and Character Map to refresh your memory.

Introduction

Beowulf probably was composed in England sometime in the eighth century AD and written down *circa* 1000 AD by a literate *scop* (bard) or perhaps a Christian scribe who was possibly educated in a monastery. The poem was created in the oral-formulaic tradition (or oral poetic method), probably developing over a period of time with roots in folk tales and traditional stories until a single, very talented poet put it in something very near its current form.

The poem would have been performed for audiences at court or on the road as the *scop* (preferred pronunciation, "shop") found audiences to support him. The *scop* would sing or chant the poem, rather than recite it, usually to the accompaniment of a harp. The *scop's* audience was probably familiar with the story and the various allusions in the poem. The poet's skill was judged by how well he could weave the stories into an effective, entertaining presentation. Performances like this are presented in *Beowulf* by Hrothgar's court *scop*, honoring Beowulf.

Note: Quotations are from Howell D. Chickering, Jr.'s dual-language (facing-page) translation, *Beowulf* (New York: Anchor Books, Doubleday, 1977), introduction and commentary by the translator. Lines quoted are simply indicated in parentheses. In the Anglo-Saxon, each line is separated into two parts by a caesura (indicated by spacing). Here, the extra spacing has been eliminated from brief quotes for the sake of simplicity.

Beowulf as Epic

Scholars debate almost everything about *Beowulf,* including the question of whether it should be considered an epic at all. An epic is a long narrative poem, composed in an elevated style, dealing with the trials and achievements of a great hero or heroes. The epic celebrates virtues of national, military, religious, cultural, political, or historical significance. The word "epic" itself comes from the Greek *epos,* originally meaning "word" but later "oration" or "song." Like all art, an epic may grow out of a limited context but achieves greatness in relation to its universality. Epics typically emphasize heroic action as well as the struggle between the hero's own ethos and his human failings or mortality.

All of these characteristics apply to *Beowulf.* The hero, Beowulf, is the title character. He represents the values of the heroic age, specifically the Germanic code of *comitatus*—the honor system that existed in Scandinavian countries in the fifth and sixth centuries between a king, or feudal lord, and his warriors (thanes). Thanes swore devotion to their leader and vowed to fight boldly, to the death if necessary, for him. If the leader should fall, his thanes must avenge his life. For his part, the leader rewarded his thanes with treasure, protection, and land. His generosity often was considered a virtue and a mark of character. Courage, loyalty, and reputation were other virtues for these warriors, and we can look for them as themes in the poem. The code of the *comitatus* is at the heart of the *Beowulf* epic.

Increasingly, scholars distinguish between two types of epic. The first, the *primary epic*, evolves from the mores, legends, or folk tales of a people and is initially developed in an *oral tradition* of story telling. *Secondary epics* are literary. They are written from their inception and designed to appear as whole stories. Under this definition, *Beowulf* is a primary epic, the best evidence being that it first existed in the oral tradition. Furthermore, *Beowulf* does employ digressions, long speeches, journeys and quests, various trials or tests of the hero, and even divine intervention, as do classic epics. We might call *Beowulf* a *folk* epic, although some scholars prefer an emphasis on its mythological background.

Beowulf, however, differs from the classic epics of ancient Greece, the *Iliad* and the *Odyssey*, which were composed some 1,500 years before and set the standard for the epic tradition. It does not open with an invocation to a Muse, and it does not start *in medias res* ("in the middle of things"), although time *is* out of joint in the poem, especially in its last third.

Some of the devices employed by the *Beowulf* poet, such as frequent digressions, may seem tedious to the modern reader. To his audience, however, the list of heroes, villains, and battles were familiar. The stories of great achievements were cherished and intended to honor Beowulf's own accomplishments. Poems like this appealed to a wide audience and constituted a form of public entertainment. In *Beowulf* itself, we witness the captivating talents of performing storytellers; an example is the *scop* who sings of *The Finnsburh Episode* (1063–1159).

Beowulf as History

One point to remember is that the poem is not history. In a way, *Beowulf*'s world runs parallel to history. Although it rarely refers to historical facts, the setting is similar to reality in Denmark and Sweden in the fifth and sixth centuries, the time of the action in the poem. The social structure of the *comitatus* did exist; and the most dominating rituals in the poem, the funerals near the beginning and at the end of the epic, have been confirmed by archaeological discovery.

The most famous of these was the Sutton Hoo dig in East Anglia in 1939. Sutton Hoo was a burial ground for one or more East Anglian kings in the early seventh century. Its contents include a ship burial reminiscent of the funeral for Scyld Scefing near the beginning of *Beowulf* and somewhat like the final resting place of Beowulf himself. Buried with the ship were various gold coins and pieces of armor, including an impressive helmet, a representation of which is used for the cover of Howell D. Chickering, Jr.'s paperback translation. Other artifacts include both pagan and Christian symbols, indicating the fusion of cultures in England approaching the time of the composition of the poem. We might remember that Pope Gregory, who served from 590 to 604, encouraged Christian missionaries to absorb pagan tradition into Christian ritual in order to promote a smooth transition for the pagans.

Royal ship burials, at sea or on land, were also part of the Scandinavian culture from at least the fifth century through the ninth. Another significant archaeological discovery was at Oseburg in southern Norway, just one of several in Scandinavia. The tribal feuds of the fifth and sixth centuries are well documented historically, and the death of King Hygelac in battle (*circa* 520) is a recorded fact.

Another custom was the concept of *wergild,* literally, "man-payment," the price set on a person's life according to his social or political station. If a lord or one of his top thanes (sometimes called a *retainer*) were killed in a feud, the fighting might go on indefinitely, one side killing for vengeance and then the other. However, the fighting could be stopped by a payment of *wergild.* If a leader were killed, the offending party could pay a certain amount to have the matter settled. Long before the opening of the poem, Hrothgar apparently made such a payment to buy Beowulf's father out of a feud, and part of Beowulf's motivation in coming to fight Grendel is to pay off this family obligation.

Still, getting too wrapped up in historical parallels is dangerous. While some things are realistic, others are not. The world in *Beowulf* is one of the imagination. We should not be too concerned about whether Beowulf can hold his breath all day or swim five nights without rest, or, for that matter, whether dragons keep treasure-troves. In *Beowulf's* world, they do.

Poetic Devices

Beowulf is an example of Anglo-Saxon poetry that is distinguished by its heavy use of alliteration. Simply put, *alliteration* is the repetition of initial sounds of words. For example, notice the initial *h* sounds in the following line: "The harrowing history haunted the heroes." In the original *Beowulf,* alliteration is used in almost every line. A line of the poem actually consists of two half-lines with a caesura (pause) between them. Usually, spacing indicates that pause. In the following example, notice how the words of the first half-line alliterate with each other and the first word of the second half-line:

839 *ferdon folc-togan feorran ond nean*

839 chieftains came from far and near

Sometimes the alliteration is more complicated and has been the subject of many advanced studies. The point for beginning students is that alliteration is as important in *Beowulf* as rhyme is for some later poets. *Beowulf* has no consistent pattern of rhyme, although occasional internal rhyme sometimes is effective and seems more than accidental.

Imagery in the poem is vivid and often fun, and frequently related through the use of *kennings*. Put simply, kennings are compound expressions that use characteristics to *name* a person or thing. One of the most popular examples is *hronrade*. Literally, the word means "whale-road"; the kenning, then, is for the sea or ocean, a thoroughfare for the whale. One of the strengths of the Chickering facing-page translation is that it often repeats the kennings literally. Sometimes even a beginning student can find the word in Anglo-Saxon, on the opposing page, for comparison. Following are some other examples of kennings:

Kenning	Literal Translation	Meaning
hand-sporu	hand spike	Grendel's talon
word-hord	word hoard	vocabulary
ban-cofan	bone box	a person's body

Another device that modern readers might notice is the use of *litotes*, which are figures of speech in which a positive statement is made by the negative of its opposite. It is a form of understatement that is none too subtle. We might say, for example, "Abraham Lincoln was not too bad a President" when we mean to convey that he was a great President. When describing Grendel's mere (or pool), King Hrothgar says (1372) it is "Not a pleasant place!" It is, in fact, filled with horror.

Although modern works often contain poetic devices such as the simile, there are only a few similes in *Beowulf. Simile* often is described as a comparison between two objects, people, or ideas through the use of a comparative such as "like" or "as." One simile occurs in line 218 when the poet tells us that the ship went over the sea "like a bird." A more original, complex, extended simile (2444 ff.) compares the feelings of King Hrethel with those of a father whose son is on the gallows, the "likeness," or similarity, implied by the first line.

As poetry, *Beowulf* is rich in meaning. Some see it as an early celebration of Christianity. Others think it extols *or* condemns heroic values. English novelist and scholar J. R. R. Tolkien ("*Beowulf:* The Monsters and the Critics," *Proceedings of the British Academy,* XXII [1936], 245–95) argued that *Beowulf* is a balance between beginnings and endings, of youth and age, the most dominating being Beowulf's. While the poem is of value historically, it is more interesting as a powerful work of art.

A Brief Synopsis

Beowulf is the longest and greatest surviving Anglo-Saxon poem. The setting of the epic is the sixth century in what is now known as Denmark and southwestern Sweden. The poem opens with a brief genealogy of the Scylding (Dane) royal dynasty, named after a mythic hero, Scyld Scefing, who reached the tribe's shores as a castaway babe on a ship loaded with treasure. Scyld's funeral is a memorable early ritual in the work, but focus soon shifts to the reign of his great-grandson, Hrothgar, whose successful rule is symbolized by a magnificent central mead-hall called Heorot. For 12 years, a huge man-like ogre named Grendel, a descendant of the biblical murderer Cain, has menaced the aging Hrothgar, raiding Heorot and killing the king's thanes (warriors). Grendel rules the mead-hall nightly.

Beowulf, a young warrior in Geatland (southwestern Sweden), comes to the Scyldings' aid, bringing with him 14 of his finest men. Hrothgar once sheltered Beowulf's father during a deadly feud, and the mighty Geat hopes to return the favor while enhancing his own reputation and gaining treasure for his king, Hygelac. At a feast before nightfall of the first day of the visit, an obnoxious, drunken Scylding named Unferth insults Beowulf and claims that the Geat visitor once embarrassingly lost a swimming contest to a boyhood acquaintance named Breca and is no match for Grendel. Beowulf responds with dignity while putting Unferth in his place. In fact, the two swimmers were separated by a storm on the fifth night of the contest, and Beowulf had slain nine sea monsters before finally returning to shore.

While the Danes retire to safer sleeping quarters, Beowulf and the Geats bed down in Heorot, fully aware that Grendel will visit them. He does. Angered by the joy of the men in the mead-hall, the ogre furiously bursts in on the Geats, killing one and then reaching for Beowulf. With the strength of 30 men in his hand-grip, Beowulf seizes the ogre's claw and does not let go. The ensuing battle nearly destroys the great hall, but Beowulf emerges victorious as he rips Grendel's claw from its shoulder socket, sending the mortally wounded beast fleeing to his mere (pool). The claw trophy hangs high under the roof of Heorot.

The Danes celebrate the next day with a huge feast featuring entertainment by Hrothgar's *scop* (pronounced "shop"), a professional bard who accompanies himself on a harp and sings or chants traditional lays such as an account of the Danes' victory at Finnsburh. This bard also improvises a song about Beowulf's victory. Hrothgar's wife, Queen Wealhtheow, proves to be a perfect hostess, offering Beowulf a gold collar and her gratitude. Filled with mead, wine, and great food, the entire party retires for what they expect to be the first peaceful night in years.

But Grendel's mother—not quite as powerful as her son but highly motivated—climbs to Heorot that night, retrieves her son's claw, and murderously abducts one of the Scyldings (Aeschere) while Beowulf sleeps elsewhere. The next morning, Hrothgar, Beowulf, and a retinue of Scyldings and Geats follow the mother's tracks into a dark, forbidding swamp and to the edge of her mere. The slaughtered Aeschere's head sits on a cliff by the lake, which hides the ogres' underground cave. Carrying a sword called *Hrunting*, a gift from the chastised Unferth, Beowulf dives into the mere to seek the mother.

Near the bottom of the lake, Grendel's mother attacks and hauls the Geat warrior to her dimly lit cave. Beowulf fights back once inside the dry cavern, but the gift sword, Hrunting, strong as it is, fails to penetrate the ogre's hide. The mother moves to kill Beowulf with her knife, but his armor, made by the legendary blacksmith Weland, protects him. Suddenly Beowulf spots a magical, giant sword and uses it to cut through the mother's spine at the neck, killing her. A blessed light unexplainably illuminates the cavern, disclosing Grendel's corpse and a great deal of treasure. Beowulf decapitates the corpse. The magic sword melts to its hilt. Beowulf returns to the lake's surface carrying the head and hilt but leaving the treasure.

After more celebration and gifts and a sermon by Hrothgar warning of the dangers of pride and the mutability of time, Beowulf and his men return to Geatland. There he serves his king well until Hygelac is killed in battle and his son dies in a feud. Beowulf is then named king and rules successfully for 50 years. Like Hrothgar, however, his peace is shattered in his declining years. Beowulf must battle one more demon.

A fiery dragon has become enraged because a lone fugitive has inadvertently discovered the dragon's treasure-trove and stolen a valuable cup. The dragon terrorizes the countryside at night, burning several homes, including Beowulf's. Led by the fugitive, Beowulf and eleven of his men seek out the dragon's barrow. Beowulf insists on taking on the dragon alone, but his own sword, Naegling, is no match for the monster. Seeing his king in trouble, one thane, Wiglaf, goes to his assistance. The others flee to the woods. Together, Wiglaf and Beowulf kill the dragon, but the mighty king is mortally wounded. Dying, Beowulf leaves his kingdom to Wiglaf and requests that his body be cremated in a funeral pyre and buried high on a seaside cliff where passing sailors might see the barrow. The dragon's treasure-hoard is buried with him. It is said that they lie there still.

List of Characters

Danes (Scyldings)

Scyld Scefing A mythical figure, Scyld was the founder of the tribe of the Scyldings long before Beowulf's story begins. His ship funeral early in the poem is a significant ritual.

Hrothgar The aging king of the Danes welcomes Beowulf's assistance in facing the menace of Grendel. His sermon to Beowulf before the Geat champion's departure is thematically important; his great mead-hall, Heorot, symbolizes the kingdom's success, civilization, and joy.

Wealhtheow Hrothgar's queen welcomes Beowulf and is the embodiment of charm and hospitality.

Unferth One of Hrothgar's top retainers, Unferth insults Beowulf after dipping too deeply into the mead bowl at the first banquet. He later lends Beowulf a sword for a crucial battle.

Geats (Weder-Folk or Weders)

Beowulf A mighty warrior and noble individual, the poem's hero, with the strength of 30 in his hand-grip, comes to the aid of Hrothgar's Danes. Later Beowulf is king of the Geats.

Wiglaf The only thane to stand with Beowulf against the dragon, he is the Geats' future king and a symbol of loyalty within the social/political structure of the *comitatus*.

Hygelac King of the Geats and uncle to Beowulf, his death in battle (c. 520) is recorded historically, unlike most of the events in the poem.

Hygd Hygelac's queen is a perfect hostess in the style of Wealhtheow and exemplifies propriety in royalty. Beowulf is loyal to her and her young son, Heardred, when Hygelac dies.

Heardred Despite Beowulf's support, the young king, son of Hygelac and Hygd, is killed in a feud. Beowulf then becomes king of the Geats.

Monsters

Grendel A descendant of the biblical Cain, the enormous ogre despises mankind's joy. He menaces Hrothgar and the Danes for 12 years before facing Beowulf in battle.

Grendel's mother Although not as powerful as her son, she is a formidable foe. She and her son live in a cave beneath a swampy lake (or mere) where she battles Beowulf.

Dragon Guarding a treasure-trove in Geatland, he is angered when a fugitive steals a single gold-plated flagon. His raids throughout the countryside lead to a battle with Beowulf, the king's last.

Two Men, Three Swords, and a Great Mead-Hall

Breca A royal member of the Brondings, he and Beowulf engaged in a swimming contest against each other as adolescents, which Unferth claims Beowulf lost.

Weland The legendary, magical blacksmith who made Beowulf's armor.

Hrunting Beowulf receives the ancient sword from Unferth and uses it, albeit unsuccessfully, against Grendel's mother.

Naegling Beowulf's own mighty sword is ineffective in the fight with the fiery dragon.

Magical Giant Sword Beowulf miraculously finds this wonderful weapon in the underwater cave and uses it to kill Grendel's mother. It melts down to the hilt after Beowulf uses it to decapitate Grendel's corpse. Beowulf presents the hilt to Hrothgar along with Grendel's head.

Heorot Hrothgar's mead-hall is more like a palace, symbolizing his and the Scyldings' success. Grendel sees it as a symbol of mankind's joy and delights in raiding and capturing it nightly.

Character Map

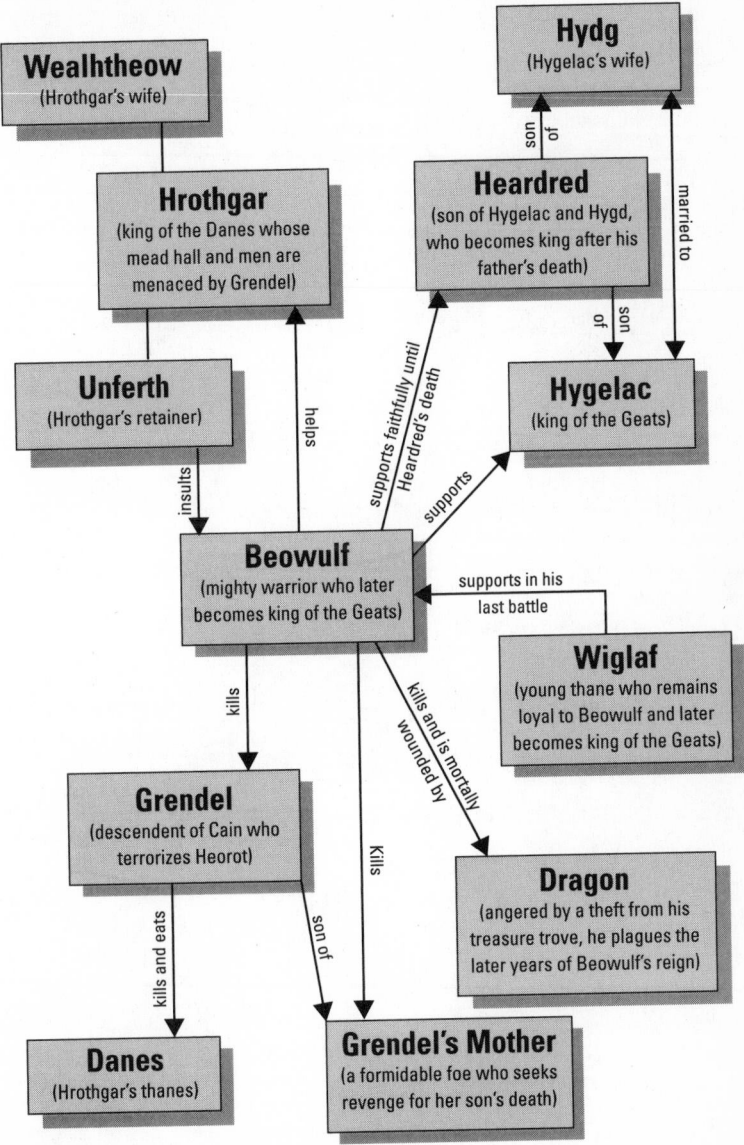

Beowulf Geography

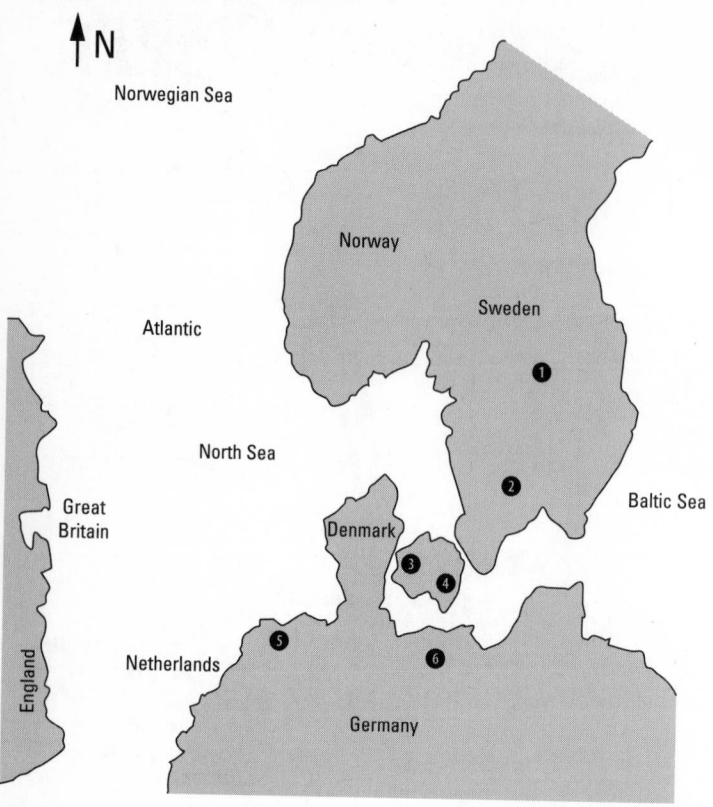

1. Swedes (Scylfings)

2. Geats

3. Danes

4. Heorot

5. Frisians

6. Heathobards

CRITICAL COMMENTARIES

The sections that follow provide great tools for supplementing your reading of Beowulf. First, in order to enhance your understanding of and enjoyment from reading, we provide quick summaries in case you have difficulty when you read the original literary work. Each summary is followed by commentary: literary devices, character analyses, themes, and so on. Keep in mind that the interpretations here are solely those of the author of this study guide and are used to jumpstart your thinking about the work. No single interpretation of a complex work like Beowulf is infallible or exhaustive, and you'll likely find that you interpret portions of the work differently from the author of this study guide. Read the original work and determine your own interpretations, referring to these Notes for supplemental meanings only.

Lines 1–193

Summary

The poem's narrator calls for the attention of his audience and introduces his topic with a brief genealogy of the Scyldings (Danes). The tribe has taken its name from Scyld Scefing, a mythological hero who, many years earlier, reached their shores as a castaway babe on a ship mysteriously laden with treasure. Through industry, courage, and character, Scyld Scefing became a great leader and honored king. His son, Beow (sometimes called Beowulf but not to be confused with the epic's central hero), continued the successful reign after Scyld's death and sea burial. Beow ruled long and well, "beloved by his people" (54). Beow's son, Healfdene, sired four offspring, the most notable of whom is Hrothgar, king of the Scyldings as the story unfolds. Hrothgar has been a great king and won many victories for his people. As a symbol of his success, he has built a great mead-hall, called Heorot, the finest of its kind. In Heorot, Hrothgar's men celebrate with joyful laughter and songs from the king's bard. The Scyldings prosper.

An ogre named Grendel lives in the nearby moors and takes exception to his neighbors' excessive happiness. A descendant of Cain, he envies and resents mankind. One night he attacks without warning and slaughters 30 of Hrothgar's men. He returns the next night and soon drives the Scyldings from the great hall. His ruthless dominance lasts 12 years.

Commentary

It is often said that *Beowulf* begins and ends with a funeral, and that is very nearly the case. The narrator sets the heroic tone and introduces the setting through the founding character of Scyld Scefing; his most detailed early description is saved for Scyld's parting after death. The king's body is placed on a ship, surrounded by treasure and "war-dress" (39) to accompany him into the unknown. Gold, silver, jewels, and the finest swords and armor are placed aboard with the corpse and then set afloat in the sea. The idea is to honor the king but also to provide him with objects that might prove useful in the afterlife.

Literary Device

Hrothgar's great hall (Heorot, "Hall of the Hart") functions as both symbol and setting. Symbolically, it represents the achievements of the Scyldings, specifically Hrothgar, and their level of civilization. It is a place of light and warmth in the dark, cold winters. Here Hrothgar celebrates his victories and rewards his thanes (warriors) with various rings and treasures. Heorot is no common beer hall; it is more of a palace, towering high like a cliff. Significantly, this is where Beowulf's first great battle for the Danes takes place. The hall also symbolizes the concept of *comitatus,* the honor code that exists between the king, or feudal lord, and his warriors. Thanes swear devotion to their leader and vow to fight boldly, to the death if necessary, for him. If the leader should fall, his life must be avenged. For his part, the leader rewards his thanes with treasure, protection, and land. His generosity often is mentioned as one of his strengths of character.

Character Insight

When Grendel invades this setting, he strikes at the very heart of the Scyldings. Grendel's heritage is essential to his enmity. He is a descendant of the biblical Cain, the eldest son of Adam and Eve who killed his brother Abel out of jealousy (Genesis 4). Cain's name in Hebrew is *Qayin*, meaning "creature," and the legend is that the monsters of the earth are his descendants. Grendel resents the joyful beauty of Heorot and its inhabitants. The *scop*'s Song of Creation (90–98) especially enrages him because it tells of the beauty and light of God's creation, which Grendel can never recover for himself.

The modern reader might think it odd that the poem's narrator interrupts his description of the glories of the hall to foreshadow (82–85) the hall's eventual destruction by Hrothgar's son-in-law, but such digressions are common in *Beowulf.* Throughout the epic are the reminders of the sometimes grim whims of fate and the mutability of human existence. The world of *Beowulf* is harsh, and joy is never permanent.

There is considerable scholarly discussion concerning the concept of Christianity in *Beowulf.* The epic makes no mention of Jesus, and references to one omnipotent God are more Old than New Testament. Harold Bloom (*Bloom's Reviews: Beowulf*, 1999, p. 5) says that the epic is a Christian poem but "just barely." Hrothgar and Beowulf sometimes refer to a single, all-powerful God; there are instances of symbolic rebirth in the epic. Grendel and his mother are described as descendants of Cain. The *Beowulf* poet may have been an educated Christian, and his audience in eighth-century England had been exposed to the religion.

But the poem is more heroic than Christian. Sometimes it seems as if Christian terms have simply replaced heroic. For example, occasional mention of God's determination regarding man's fortune, throughout the poem, sounds very much like the Anglo-Saxon concept of fate *(wyrd)*.

This heroic/Christian world is the context for Grendel who "grieved not at all / for his wicked deeds" (136–37) as well as the thanes who "were ignorant of God, / knew not how to worship our Protector above" (181–82). Grendel is too deeply engrossed in sin to consider repentance. He is beyond hope. The thanes are pagan and near despair themselves as Grendel decimates them. They offer sacrifices to heathen gods and speak old words designed to ward off evil. Some scholars argue that the warriors are Christian but "backsliding" to pagan ritual under stress. At any rate, nothing works. Hrothgar and his men abandon the glorious hall at night, and it becomes Grendel's lair. Only the "gift-throne" (168), Hrothgar's seat of power, cannot be touched by Grendel because it carries God's blessing. Hrothgar has grown old and is helpless against Grendel. He needs "the strongest of all living men" (196) to rescue him.

Glossary

(Here and in the following sections, difficult words and phrases, as well as allusions and historical references, are explained.)

Spear-Danes Scyldings, the tribe of Scyld Scefing.

waif a forsaken or orphaned child, such as Scyld.

whale-road ocean or sea, from the Anglo-Saxon *hron-rade*. This is one of the poem's best known *kennings,* descriptive metaphors that identify a person or thing by a chief characteristic or use.

Life-lord God.

ring-giver ruler, king, feudal lord.

Scylfing Swede.

mead an alcoholic drink made from fermented honey and water.

middle-earth a land between Heaven and Hell, inhabited by mankind as well as a variety of good or evil creatures with origins in legend, mythology, or fantasy.

scop a bard or singing (chanting) performer who often accompanies himself on a lute or harp, presenting historical or legendary stories of interest. He might be attached to a court or travel on his own. Preferred pronunciation is "shop."

walking dead similar to zombies, cursed to roam the earth after death.

thanes warriors who serve a king or feudal lord in exchange for land or treasure.

warlock male witch or demon.

Lines 194–606

Summary

In the land of the Geats, today southwestern Sweden, the most powerful of all living warriors—Beowulf—hears of Hrothgar's dilemma. A nephew and thane of King Hygelac, Beowulf carefully chooses 14 of the finest warriors in Geatland to sail to Denmark. A retainer of Hrothgar, assigned to guarding the coast, spots Beowulf and his men when they land and leads the group to Heorot. Almost everyone is impressed with Beowulf's noble stature, enormous size, and obvious strength. Hrothgar's herald, Wulfgar, strongly urges the king to meet with Beowulf and the Geats. Hrothgar needs little convincing. He once protected Beowulf's now deceased father, Ecgtheow, from a blood feud and knew Beowulf when he was a boy. Hrothgar has already heard that Beowulf has the strength of 30 men in his hand-grip and welcomes the visitors.

Beowulf confirms to Hrothgar that he is there to do battle with the ogre who terrorizes Heorot. The young warrior states his credentials: He has destroyed a tribe of giants, defeated sea monsters in night fight, and returned from battle covered with the blood of his enemies. He has driven trouble out of his native land. Beowulf states that he will fight Grendel without armor or sword, hand to claw, because the ogre does not use weapons. If Beowulf is killed, he wants his war-shirt (breast armor, mail) returned to King Hygelac. Hrothgar offers a joyful feast in honor of Beowulf's arrival. The good cheer is interrupted by Unferth, a top thane of Hrothgar, who insults Beowulf and questions his reputation.

Commentary

Beowulf's motives for sailing to Denmark are complex. First, he is a young warrior eager to earn glory and enhance his reputation. He can expect to be rewarded well if he is victorious. Second, he is on a lifelong quest of honor; only through fame and honor can a warrior hope to gain a measure of immortality. Finally, and probably most importantly, there is an implication that Beowulf's family owes a debt to

Hrothgar. Beowulf's father, Ecgtheow, once killed a leader of another tribe in a feud. When his enemies sought vengeance, Ecgtheow took refuge with Hrothgar, then a young king. Eventually, Hrothgar settled the feud by making a tribute payment *(wergild)* of "fine old treasures" (472) to Ecgtheow's enemies. The bond between the families goes back many years, and Beowulf is proud to be able to come to Hrothgar's assistance.

Beowulf is an impressive-looking man. The reader first encounters him as he disembarks from the ship. The coastal guard points out that he has never seen "a mightier noble, / a larger man" (247–48) even though he has held this watch and seen many warriors come and go. Beowulf is huge and strong. He carries himself with the bearing of a noble leader, a champion. He is a young man, probably in his early twenties.

Theme

Reputation is one of the major themes of the epic. As the coastal guard first approaches the Geats, he asks about Beowulf's lineage (251)—the same question that a visitor might expect in the Greek epic, *The Odyssey,* composed some 1,500 years before. Beowulf responds by itemizing his father's accomplishments and reputation. He briefly mentions his king, Hygelac, and his people, the Geats. When Beowulf lists his own accomplishments to Hrothgar (418 ff.), he is respecting custom rather than indulging in vanity. Hrothgar wants to know more about the man who has come to rescue him. Beowulf has properly held back information about himself while dealing with a mere coastal guard but details his personal reputation to the king.

Beowulf's decision to fight Grendel without a weapon has a touch of irony. Although he may be motivated by a sense of fair play, as well as a touch of pride, Beowulf is *unknowingly* doing himself a favor when he chooses to confront the ogre without a sword. We later learn that Grendel is protected by a magic spell and cannot be injured by man's weapons. But Beowulf does not know this. In a very practical sense, Beowulf's desire for honest glory protects him. He follows this pronouncement with a humble recognition of his possible defeat by Grendel. The graphic details of that possibility, along with Hrothgar's gory description (484 ff.) of the mead-hall after his own warriors were slaughtered by Grendel, underline the seriousness of Beowulf's undertaking.

One of Hrothgar's top retainers, Unferth, interrupts the celebration to insult Beowulf and challenge his reputation. When Beowulf was a youth, apparently during his adolescence, he engaged in a swimming match on the open sea with another boy, named Breca. Unferth asserts that Beowulf was vain and foolish to enter such a dangerous contest and that Breca proved the stronger, defeating Beowulf in seven nights. If Beowulf couldn't win a swimming match, Unferth concludes, then he is surely no match for Grendel, who, in addition to presenting formidable physical challenge, lives in a lake or at the bottom of a lake. Swimming may prove essential if Beowulf is forced to pursue the enemy.

Character Insight

Beowulf's response to Unferth reveals a good deal about the hero's noble character and is a remarkable example of rhetoric as well as poetic imagery. Beowulf's response is composed and in control. First he isolates the problem; Unferth has been dipping deeply into the mead bowl: "What a great deal, Unferth my friend, / full of beer, you have said about Breca, / told of his deeds" (530–532). Having addressed the issue, Beowulf calmly but strongly counters Unferth's factual assertions. He concedes that, as boys will do (at least boys in Geatland), he and Breca exchanged boasts and entered into a dangerous swimming contest on the open sea. They wore body armor for protection, and each carried a sword. They swam together five nights, not seven. Breca could not pull away, and Beowulf would not abandon the other boy. Rough seas finally drove them apart. Sea monsters attacked Beowulf and attempted to drag him down. By dawn, he had killed nine of them. Fate *(Wyrd)* saved him, but only because it was not his time and he had fought courageously.

Beowulf then turns the speech back to Unferth, asserting wryly that he has never heard of any similar achievement by his accuser. He has, however, heard that Unferth has killed his own brothers, for which he will be condemned to Hell even though he may be "clever" with words. (We are reminded of Cain, another brother-killer, and the damnation that descends even to Grendel.) With that, Beowulf directly addresses the problems that the Scyldings have had with Grendel. Raising his rhetoric a notch, he shames Unferth by saying that Grendel would not have been so successful against King Hrothgar if Unferth's "battle-spirit, were as sharp as your words" (596). In his conclusion, Beowulf sardonically refers to the "Victory-Scyldings" (597), still directing his speech to Unferth, and concludes that Grendel has no fear of *him*. However, a Geat, Beowulf, will defeat the ogre. The next day, Unferth and his friends will be able to "walk brave to mead" (604).

Beowulf has gone just far enough. He has shown admirable restraint without backing down, and his verbal attacks have been centered on Unferth, not the Scyldings generally. King Hrothgar and the others applaud and laugh. The speech is a huge success.

The poetic imagery of the passage is worth notice as well, especially when the poet associates the metaphor of feasting with death. Beowulf says that the denizens of the deep intended to feast on him, amusingly suggesting a scene in which sea-beasts are formally pulling up to a banquet on the ocean floor. Instead, he offers them a "sword-feast" (562); they eat death. The crisis of Unferth's insult has passed. It is nothing compared to the challenge that is about to come.

Glossary

Geats also called Weder-Folk or Weders. This is Beowulf's tribe in southwestern Sweden.

eddy a current running contrary to the main current, sometimes producing whirlpools.

retainer an attendant to the king, here sometimes used interchangeably with "thane."

mail flexible armor made of small, overlapping rings or scales.

lineage ancestry, background, heritage.

word-hoard a kenning for *vocabulary.*

shield of the people here, a reference to King Hrothgar.

Weders Geats.

gold-laced hall Heorot.

Weland in Germanic legend, a blacksmith with magical powers; he made Beowulf's war-shirt (455).

Lapps inhabitants of northern Scandinavia and Finland. The Anglo-Saxon is *"Finna land"* (580).

Lines 607–836

Summary

As the good will of the gathering returns, Queen Wealhtheow passes around more mead. Courteous and stately, adorned with gold and jewels, she makes an impressive appearance. She greets Beowulf and thanks God for his arrival. Beowulf pledges to defeat Grendel that night in the mead-hall or die trying. Hrothgar retires early. The party breaks up, but Beowulf and the Geats remain to spend the night in Heorot.

Grendel comes up from the marsh hoping to find a human to devour. In some respects, he looks like a man: two arms (something like giant claws), two legs, one head; but he is much larger and stronger than most men and might be thought of as a huge, angry monster whose joy is destroying the joy of men. He is delighted when he sees several Geats sleeping in the hall. Beowulf lies awake, watching, as Grendel kills and eats one of the warriors. Then he reaches for his second kill, Beowulf. The Geat champion grabs hold of Grendel's claw with the strength of 30 men and won't let go. Grendel cannot escape, and a vicious match ensues, ending when Beowulf rips Grendel's arm from its shoulder socket. Mortally wounded, Grendel flees. Beowulf hangs the giant's claw under the roof of the mead-hall (926–983).

Commentary

Theme

Hospitality and generosity are major themes in *Beowulf*, and Wealhtheow is their most gracious representative. Wealhtheow is the perfect host. She is beautiful and richly attired, courteous, proper, and "excellent in virtues" (623). Following decorum, she offers the first cup of mead to King Hrothgar, her husband. She then proceeds through the hall, serving as she goes, but pays special attention to Beowulf, greeting him appropriately and thanking God for sending the great warrior. Apparently touched by the queen's grace, Beowulf vows that he will end that night with either victory over Grendel or his own death.

The role of women is limited in the epic; they were still thought of as chattel, possessions of their husbands. Among the nobility, however, they sometimes were used as peacemakers. Feuding tribes might find it in their best interests to unite through marriage. There is an indication that Queen Wealhtheow came to Hrothgar as a result of that kind of union. The novelist and scholar John Gardner makes more of that in *his* fictional account of the tale, titled *Grendel* (1971) and told sympathetically from the point of view of the ogre. Wealhtheow is from a Germanic tribe, a Helming or Wylfing. A connection like that could have aided Hrothgar when he bought a truce for Beowulf's father (470). Hrothgar has also sought peace with the Heathobards, another Germanic tribe, by giving his daughter in marriage to Prince Ingeld; this attempt fails when the Heathobards destroy Heorot, a future event referred to ominously by the *Beowulf* poet.

When Hrothgar retires for the night, he comments that this is the first night that he has ever entrusted the care of his hall to another man. Heorot is the symbol of his rule. In effect, Hrothgar is placing his reign in Beowulf's mighty hands. Significantly, he tells Beowulf to remember *fame*. Although the poet frequently mentions God, these warriors' credo is really devoted to glory, reputation, honor, wealth, and fame. The modern reader might benefit from understanding that fame and reputation are close to the same thing in Beowulf's world.

Style & Language

Beowulf strips for bed, noting again (677 ff.) that he will not use weapons against Grendel because the ogre "does not know the warrior's arts" (681), the skills of a fighter trained in the use of weapons. Although this is called a "boast" (676), it sounds more like another vow. Beowulf sets aside his chain-shirt. When the poet tells us that the "pillow took the cheek" (688) of the mighty warrior, he is pointing out that Beowulf wears no protective helmet even though the Geat champion is sure that Grendel will come.

Literary Device

And come he does. In a passage that almost everyone agrees is one of the finest in Anglo-Saxon poetry (710–727), Grendel ascends from the fen. The poetry here is best appreciated if read aloud in Old English with a literal understanding of each word. (Chickering's "Glosses to Select Passages" (p. 397–98) include translations.) In set stages, Grendel approaches the "house of . . . joy to men" (715–16). Angry, defiant, and cursed, Grendel resents, above all, the hope and happiness of mankind. The poet effectively contrasts the light of Heorot with the darkness of the fen and Grendel's soul. One metaphor for killing warriors is to drag them into the "shadows" (707), which even the ogre cannot accomplish if it is not God's will. Grendel comes "up from the marsh, under misty cliffs" (710), a demon ascending from a dark hell. The night is noticeably dark as he approaches the "shining wine-hall" (715) where the Geats wait. The only brightness coming from Grendel is "an ugly light [that] shone out [from his eyes] like fire" (727).

Literary
Device

The door to Heorot bursts open at the ogre's touch, implying Grendel's great strength. His heart laughs, an effective metaphor, at the sight of the sleeping Geats. Grendel's entrance into Heorot anticipates his brutality. He doesn't just knock down the door; he "rip[s] open / the mouth of the hall" (723–24). In a device often used by the poet, this image anticipates the next major action: Grendel's ripping apart of the Geat warrior, Hondscio (740 ff.). Grendel quickly guts the man while the warrior still sleeps. Blood swills from veins ripped open by the ogre's mouth, and the warrior is quickly devoured. With an appreciation for gruesome detail, the poet reveals that Grendel even gulps down *"fet ond folma"* (745), the feet and hands of the Geat.

Meanwhile, Beowulf watches, learning the likely approach of his adversary. Some critics complain that Beowulf should attack immediately instead of observing as his man dies, but A. K. Moore (*Modern Language Notes* 68 [1953], 165–69) has it right when he points out that Beowulf's responsibility lies in the *mission*, not the protection of one warrior. When Grendel reaches for Beowulf, the world's strongest human hand grips the ogre and won't let go. Although Grendel would prefer escape, he is trapped and must engage the hero.

Literary
Device

Imagery throughout the poem is specific and vivid, but it is especially strong in Beowulf and Grendel's battle sequence. The battle is furious. The two nearly knock down the superbly fortified Heorot. Danes around the compound are riveted to the noise but stay their distance. The Geats try to come to Beowulf's aid but find that their swords are ineffective because Grendel is protected from weapons by a magic spell. He must be killed by hand, and he is in the hands of the mightiest warrior alive. Instead of minutely detailing what the two combatants do to each other, the poet describes the *effect*. Mighty Heorot is nearly destroyed. We can see it almost bursting. The fixtures are in ruins. Ornate mead benches are ripped from the floor. Grendel's scream of hate and pain horrifies the Danes who prudently remain well outside the hall.

The poet then zeroes in on a very specific piece of the action. Beowulf tears Grendel's arm from its shoulder. Tendons pop. The bone-locker bursts (*"burston ban-locan,"* 818) as muscles are ripped away. Here the imagery takes the reader very close. Mortally wounded, Grendel flees back into the darkness. Triumphantly, Beowulf hangs the trophy under the high roof.

Glossary

Bright-Danes another name for the Scyldings, the reference to shining light.

Helmings Wealhtheow's original tribe.

King of Glory God, not Hrothgar.

body-warden a kenning for a chain-mail shirt.

shepherd of sins Grendel, perhaps in contrast to God as shepherd of souls.

fen low, swampy land.

palisade a defensive fortification or fence made of pointed sticks (pales).

protector of nobles Beowulf.

killer-guest Grendel. The poet ironically plays with the theme of hospitality.

Lines 837–1062

Summary

Warriors and chieftains from considerable distances gather at Heorot the next morning to marvel at the trophy, Grendel's claw, and to celebrate Beowulf's victory. Some follow the ogre's bloody footprints down to his lake where the water boils with Grendel's blood. On the way back to Heorot, Hrothgar's *scop* entertains the men with traditional songs as well as an improvised account of Beowulf's victory. Included is the story of Sigemund, an ancient hero who is recalled in honor of Beowulf. In contrast, the *scop* also sings of Heremod, a bad ruler who brought sorrow and death to his own people. Hrothgar gives a speech from the porch at Heorot and thanks God for Beowulf's triumph. Beowulf briefly recounts the battle, and even Unferth is impressed enough to keep silent. Work is begun to refurbish Heorot. A great feast is held in Beowulf's honor at which Beowulf and his men receive numerous gifts.

Commentary

Theme

One of the themes of the poem is that man's fortunes change, and he should celebrate but take care when fortune seems to turn his way because disaster may visit soon. One must not tempt the gods of irony. The Geats and Danes unwisely assume that victory is complete with the death of Grendel. For now, however, everything is celebration. Warriors who trembled and hid from Grendel boldly track his footprints to the lake where he apparently has died. Scholars delight in the account of the *scop*'s performance and his improvisation on the way back to Heorot. He tells the "great old stories" (869) in honor of

Beowulf's victory, including the tale of courageous Sigemund, whose killing of the dragon foreshadows Beowulf's final battle and his death. The *Beowulf* poet thus subtly implies that all glory is fleeting and that death waits for all (1002 ff.). The *scop*'s account of Heremod appears to be in contrast to Sigemund and a reminder of what can happen when a king goes bad. All of this is part of a *celebration*.

Back at Heorot, Hrothgar's praise of God, and only secondarily Beowulf, may seem intrusive in what is predominantly a heroic story. Some scholars feel that this passage indicates tampering or, at the very least, a genuflection by the poet or scribe who was ostensibly a Christian and probably educated by the Church. Beowulf's response mentions the will of God but frankly recounts his own courage. His only regret is that he could not present the king with a complete ogre body as trophy. His account drips with irony rather than gore, depicting the struggle in terms of hospitality. He wanted to "welcome my enemy" (969) with a firm handshake but was granted only a "visitor's token" (971), rather than a full corpse, when Grendel left "that dear gift" (973), his giant claw—a kind of macabre gratuity for services rendered.

The refurbishing of Heorot is interesting in its emphasis on brightness and light. In a land (Scandinavia) where winter is cold and dark while summer is unusually bright, it is understandable that light has a positive connotation. Beowulf has just mentioned "bright God" (979). God *is* light. Goodness is bright and shining in the poem. Grendel and the fen are dark and evil. Inside refurbished Heorot, the tapestry gleams; gold weaving shines on the walls; pictures shift in the light; the building itself shines.

Character Insight

Hrothgar's generosity is an indication of his character. Of course, he has much for which to be grateful. Although aged and no match for Grendel, his gifts to Beowulf and the other Geats are splendid. Beowulf receives a golden banner, helmet, and mail-shirt as well as a jeweled sword. All the items are laced with gold. In addition, he receives eight magnificent horses, with golden trappings that hang to the floor, and a gem-studded saddle. The other Geats receive various valuable heirlooms. The poet assures us of the generosity of the gifts.

Glossary

mere a small lake or marsh.

two seas apparently the Baltic and the Atlantic; possibly the Baltic and the North Sea.

Waelsing reference to Sigemund, son of Waels.

Fitela nephew of Sigemund, possibly his bastard son.

Heremod Danish king who ruled disgracefully before Scyld rose to power.

hand-spike a kenning referring to the nail on Grendel's claw.

battle-talon another reference to Grendel's claw.

guest-house Heorot.

flagon a vessel for holding mead or other alcoholic liquids, usually made of metal or pottery and featuring a spout as well as a handle.

Hrothulf son of Halga, nephew of Hrothgar.

Ingwines another name for the Danes, literally "friends of Ing."

Lines 1063–1250

Summary

As the celebration continues within Heorot, Hrothgar's *scop* honors Beowulf with a story of another Danish victory, the Finnsburh episode.

Commentary

The inclusion of the story of Finnsburh is interesting partly because it gives us an idea of how a story like the *Beowulf* epic might have been presented. Although a modern audience might think that the *Beowulf* poet is interrupting the story, the *scop*'s performance, or something like it, probably would have taken place. Our only knowledge of the Finns-burh episode comes from two sources: *Beowulf* (lines 1068–1159 of the epic) and *The Finnsburh Fragment*, a short (47 lines) heroic ballad by another poet. The latter consists of an account of a single battle that supposedly took place in the Danes' past but recently enough to stir passions and reflect on current feuds. Critics differ on motivation of the major characters; but, considering both sources, we can make a fair assessment of the action and how it fits in *Beowulf.*

As the story begins, about 60 warriors of the Half-Danes, a division of the Danes, are visiting King Finn of Frisia at his fortress or *burh*. King Hnaef leads the Half-Danes. Hnaef's sister, Hildeburh, is married to King Finn. The marriage was probably arranged to settle a feud, which relates to *Beowulf* in that it anticipates Hrothgar's plans for his daughter (Freawaru) and may echo the reason for Hrothgar's own marriage to Wealhtheow. Queen Hildeburh and King Finn have at least one son. With the Half-Danes is Hnaef's top retainer, Hengest. These are the major players.

For motives that are not made clear, the Frisians attack the hall where the Half-Danes are sleeping. Many warriors are killed, including Hilde-burh's brother, King Hnaef (leader of the Half-Danes), and her son (a Frisian). The queen's grief is immense. This had been a place of great happiness for her. Finn's troops are so decimated that he cannot con-tinue to attack the hall; the Danes, on the other hand, are on foreign soil and unable to break out to victory.

A truce is reached, and Finn offers to take in Hnaef's thanes as his own. The Half-Danes agree out of necessity; they are on foreign soil, without a king. Old enmities and recent deaths lead to an uneasy truce. The Danes are forced to stay the winter because of rough, icy seas. As time passes, Hengest, Hnaef's top thane and now the Half-Danes' leader, thinks more about vengeance than he does about returning home. In the spring, one of the Danish warriors presents him with a sword symbolic of leadership and implying revenge.

Style & Language

The ensuing battle is introduced with the understatement of transition but specific imagery that we've grown to expect from the *Beowulf* poet: "The hall was decorated / with the lives of the foe" (1151–52), a "tapestry of blood" (1152) as Chickering translates. The Half-Danes triumph. King Finn is killed along with his men. The Danes return home with Hildeburh and assorted treasures.

Literary Device

Wealhtheow's appearance immediately follows the Finnsburh performance and reminds the poet's knowledgeable audience that she will suffer loss of family as does Queen Hildeburh in the *scop*'s story, once more foreshadowing future tragedy during current celebration. Beowulf sits between her two sons at the feast, and she asks him to serve as their good counsel and exemplar. Wealhtheow presents Beowulf with various gifts, including the largest gold collar ever seen.

Peace and joy seem to have come to Heorot. The thanes drink a great deal and fall asleep assured, for the first time in years, that they are safe in the hall. Hrothgar retires to his quarters, and Beowulf spends the night away from the hall. One visitor has not yet arrived. She will bring death to Heorot.

Glossary

Healfdene father of Hrothgar.

the giants here a reference to the Frisians.

Hoc father of Hildeburh and Hnaef.

the web's short measure the web of life—destiny, fate, *Wyrd*—has spun a short life for Queen Hildeburh's brother and son.

the prince's thane here, a reference to Hengest.

Folcwalda father of Finn.

the lord who had killed their own ring-giver an apparent reference to Finn, although it is not clear whether he personally does the killing or even if treachery is involved.

chief of the War-Scyldings Hnaef.

feud-bites a kenning for *wounds*.

Hunlaf's son a Half-Dane warrior who presents the sword to Hengest.

Guthlaf and Oslaf Half-Dane thanes.

uncle and nephew (1164) apparently a reference to Hrothgar and Hrothulf.

Hama, Brosing, and Eormanric For a thorough discussion of the necklace and the Goths, see Chickering, pp. 331–333.

Frankish pertaining to the Franks, a Germanic tribe in the Rhine region.

Lines 1251–1491

Summary

On the night following Grendel's death, the warriors sleep easy in Heorot for the first time in years, confident that the terror of the ogre is behind them. They don't realize that Grendel has a living mother intent on revenge. She ascends from her mere and raids the hall, retrieving Grendel's claw and murderously abducting one of the thanes. Before dawn, Beowulf and his men report to Hrothgar. The Geat hero agrees to pursue Grendel's mother. Hrothgar promises more rewards and greater fame for Beowulf. Accompanied by warriors, Hrothgar leads Beowulf to the mere that harbors the vengeful mother. It is a dark and evil place. Huge serpents and water-beasts inhabit the lake. Beowulf dresses for battle and prepares to search the lake for the enemy. Unferth humbles himself by presenting Beowulf with his great sword, Hrunting. The Geat hero speaks what may be his final words.

Commentary

Theme

Grendel's mother embodies the theme of revenge as she buries her grief in an assault on Heorot. Again the *Beowulf* poet reminds us that she is a descendant of Cain; but there is something very human about her motivation, which John Gardner explores compassionately in his novel *Grendel* (1971). Although she is smaller and weaker than her son and lacks his magical protection from weapons, she is determined to avenge his death and retrieve the gruesome trophy that hangs under Heorot's roof. Once in the hall, she faces a number of warriors who, in force, probably can defeat her. She grabs one, Aeschere, Hrothgar's "dearest warrior" (1296) and chief adviser. Carrying the man as well as her son's arm, she retreats to the mere.

Beowulf is once more challenged by the possibility of increased reward—treasure and fame—and is further motivated by his devotion to Hrothgar. In his pre-dawn meeting with the king, Beowulf is informed of a rumor that has, for years, suggested the existence of two ogres, one possibly in the shape of a woman. Their den reportedly is hidden in a dark mere deep within "high wolf-country" (1357), a secret place amid wind-swept cliffs and "frost-bound trees" (1364).

Style & Language

The poet's description of the mere and its surroundings is especially eerie and effective. The imagery is specific, powerful, and dark. We are told that not even the wisest of humans knows what is at the bottom of the lake. The lake is so forbidding that a hart, chased by savage hounds, will die facing the dogs rather than seek safety by plunging into the water. "Not a pleasant place!" says the poet in classic understatement (an example of litotes). In fact, this place is very *evil*. The mere is "overhung with roots that sag and clutch" (1363); it seems to burst into flame at night, portending evil and reminding the audience of the *ugly* light that "shone out like fire" (727) from Grendel's eyes. In contrast to the joyful light of Heorot, here the hills are dark; black waves erupt from the mere; a "gloomy wind / stirs awful storms till the air turns choking, / the heavens weep" (1374–76).

When Hrothgar and his retinue accompany Beowulf to the mere, easily following the mother's footprints, the poet's description is again specific and forbidding as the party enters a cold, gray, "joyless wood" (1416). Adding to the horror is the discovery of Aeschere's head on a cliff near the lake. The lake bubbles with Aeschere's blood. The mother apparently has swum with the body to an underwater hideout, some sort of waterless cavern or den whose entrance is through the mere.

Character Insight

Unferth's presentation of his treasured sword, Hrunting, to Beowulf is an admission of the Geat's superior courage and ability. So insulting when full of mead at the earlier banquet, Unferth now is all humility. Despite his obnoxious behavior at Heorot when Beowulf first arrived, we have been told that Unferth cares as much about "famous deeds" (505) and his own fame as any warrior. Now his reputation is permanently damaged because he lacks the courage to pursue the mother: "he lost fame for that" (1470).

Beowulf is not as concerned with sportsmanship as he was in the battle with Grendel. He wears his mail-shirt and helmet and carries weapons. Although the mother is less powerful than Grendel, the battle will be on her turf, a strange environment. And she is highly motivated by revenge.

Beowulf's final words before diving into the unknown of the lake are realistic. He has earlier said (1384–89) that it is better to avenge a friend than to mourn; each must face his mortality and win whatever reputation he can before death. Now (1474 ff.) he asks Hrothgar to send to Beowulf's king, Hygelac, any treasure bestowed to the Geat if he should not return from this battle. Beowulf is ready for the battle. Again, he seeks the fame of victory or death.

Glossary

abysm of time a reference to the hellish chaos, the unfathomable chasm that spawned Grendel's mother and other descendants of Cain.

Ring-Danes the Scyldings.

Ingwines another name for the Scyldings.

Yrmenlaf a Dane, Aeschere's younger brother.

rune-counselor an advisor especially adept at solving difficult problems.

unsouled The soul was believed to leave the body shortly after death.

bone-house a kenning for the body.

venom-twigs Some scholars suggest that Hrunting's edge was equipped with small, sharp points to which poison may have been applied; more likely, this is a reference to the use of acid (poison) in the shaping of the points during manufacture, a customary procedure of the time.

son of Ecglaf Unferth.

Hrethel father of King Hygelac, the Geat to whom Beowulf owes ultimate allegiance.

Lines 1492–1650

Summary

Beowulf dives into the mere wearing his mail-shirt and carrying Hrunting in its scabbard. Deep in the lake, the mother grasps him tightly with her claws so that he cannot draw his sword. The mail-shirt protects him even though various water-beasts thrust at him as the mother carries Beowulf to an underwater cave, which is dry and lighted by "glaring flames" (1517). Once there, Beowulf manages to mount an attack, but Hrunting is ineffective against the ogre's tough hide. Beowulf then tries to wrestle her, but he fails to gain the kind of death grip that defeated Grendel.

Although she is knocked down, the mother immediately counters Beowulf's attack and soon is sitting on him. She pulls her knife, but it cannot pierce his mail-shirt. Again on his feet, Beowulf spots a huge sword made by giants. Although he can barely lift it, he manages a mighty blow that severs the mother's spine at the neck, killing her. A blessed light suddenly illuminates the cavern, revealing Grendel's corpse. Beowulf lops off the head to replace the trophy of the claw that the mother retrieved.

Amazingly, the giant sword melts except for the hilt, which Beowulf carries along with Grendel's head as he returns to the surface of the mere. Only his Geats await him. Thinking him dead, Hrothgar and the Danes have returned to Heorot.

Commentary

Beowulf is resolute, and his courage is never in question. Having no sure knowledge of what he will find, he dives into the mere dressed for battle. Scholars disagree about the meaning of the line indicating that Beowulf swam down "most of the day before he found bottom" (1496). As Chickering points out in a thorough consideration of the scholarship of the section (pp. 337–341), the lines from the Anglo-Saxon literally are translated, "[T]hen it was the time of [a] day before he could find the bottom" (1495–96). One way of looking at this is that it is simply daytime, daylight, when he approaches the bottom of the lake and encounters Grendel's mother. (Readers should beware of worrying overmuch about the literal, realistic possibilities of certain events and keep in mind that the poet uses certain devices—he likes the number "30"—to indicate significant measure.)

Grendel's mother has ruled the mere for "a hundred winters" (1498)—or a *long* time. She knows the territory. Only Beowulf's mail-shirt, made by the legendary blacksmith Weland, saves him from injury as she hauls him to her cave at the bottom of the mere. Neither her grip nor the "strange sea creatures / with sword-like tusks" can do him harm. The vaulted cavern, which has served as a hideaway for Grendel and his mother, is dry and lighted only by a *glaring* blaze (1517) that reminds the audience of the "ugly light" (727) that shines like fire from Grendel's eyes. It is, perhaps, a fire from Hell that lights the cave of Cain's descendants.

Like Excalibur, Hrunting is one of many special swords of legend, which Unferth inherited and gives to Beowulf as a token of the Geat warrior's superiority. We are told that Hrunting has never failed its own-ers until now, when it cannot pierce the hide of Grendel's mother. Then Beowulf notices "a victory-bright blade / made by the giants" (1557–58) waiting in the cave. Little more is said of this blade's origins, except that the poet notes that no other mere man ever carried a sword of this length or weight into battle.

The "victory-bright blade" is just what Beowulf needs, and here the reader needs to consider, for just a moment, God's intervention. In this sequence, the *Beowulf* poet apparently has a Christian God *control* the outcome after Beowulf breaks free from the mother and stands on his own. Students may want to question whether this intervention is part of a Christian theme throughout the section (or the whole epic) or whether it is intrusive. Whether it adds to or detracts from the action is a matter of perspective. The best of critics have debated the point. At any rate, the sword is there, and in a life-or-death move, Beowulf takes one mighty swing at the mother and cuts through her spine, killing her.

Perhaps miraculously, the cave fills with brightness, "even as from heaven comes the shining light / of God's candle" (1571–72). The reader is again reminded of the motif of dark versus light, the darkness of the swamp and the light of Heorot, the dark of *evil* and the light of *goodness* in the epic. This light, whatever its source, also serves a practical purpose: Beowulf is able to explore the cave. Among various treasures, his most valuable find is the corpse of Grendel. With vengeance, Beowulf chops off the ogre's head. Eschewing all the other treasure, Beowulf leaves the cave and swims up through the mere taking only Grendel's head and the hilt of the giant sword.

On the surface of the marsh, things have changed. When blood began seeping up to the top of the mere, "a churning foam" (1593), Hrothgar and the Danes despaired of Beowulf's ever surviving and returned to Heorot. Only the Geats remain to keep a desperate vigil, wishing with no real hope that their leader would triumph. Beowulf emerges to a hero's welcome. The Geats help him out of his armor and joyfully march him back to Heorot. It takes four men to carry Grendel's head on a war-spear. The gruesome trophy makes quite an impression in the mead-hall.

Glossary

kingdom of waters here, simply a reference to the mere and the ogres' hideaway.

the lord of those rings Beowulf, with a reference to the rings that form his mail-shirt.

battle-flame the sword, Hrunting.

burnished polished until glossy.

The bold Scylding the poet associates Beowulf with the Scyldings, perhaps out of respect for his loyal service, even though the champion is a Geat.

the shearer of life-threads the magical giant sword.

gray-bearded elders Hrothgar's senior advisors.

the ninth hour the "nones," the ninth hour after sunrise, 3 p.m. As Chickering points out (p. 338), this is "the same hour that Christ, abandoned by all but a faithful few, died on the cross (see Luke 23:44–46)."

protector of sailors Beowulf.

Lines 1651–1887

Summary

Beowulf presents Grendel's head to Hrothgar and briefly recounts his battle with the mother. Assuring the king of Heorot's safety, he places the gold hilt of the giant sword in Hrothgar's hand. The king examines the hilt and then speaks to Beowulf, giving a sermon on the dangers of fame and success and the vicissitudes of life. Hrothgar notes that he himself had great fortune as a young man and ruled successfully for 50 years until Grendel brought him down. Now he thanks God for Beowulf's victory. The warriors feast and sleep safely. In the morning, Beowulf returns Hrunting to Unferth and receives numerous gifts before he and his men exchange farewells with the Danes and sail for home.

Commentary

Theme

The themes of fame (sometimes best thought of as reputation) and, even more, generosity dominate this section as Hrothgar warns Beowulf of the dangers of the former and the virtues of the latter. It may seem odd to a modern reader that the celebration of his outstanding victory should be interrupted by a solemn sermon by Hrothgar, a king who was unable to protect his own people. Nevertheless, Beowulf respects the wisdom of the aging king and patiently listens.

The trophy of Grendel's head is more satisfying to Beowulf and more valuable to him than the riches that he might have retrieved from the cave of the ogres because of the important achievement that it symbolizes. Beowulf also presents Hrothgar with the "strange gold hilt" (1677) of the giant sword. This trophy, along with Beowulf's account of its magic, seems to bring on the king's reflective mood. We are informed that the hilt's engravings tell the story of "the origin of past strife, when the flood drowned, / the pouring ocean killed the race of giants" (1689–90). There are also runes on the hilt revealing the identity of the first owner. Hrothgar considers the ephemerality of human existence and the vanity of earthly achievement. His mood seems to silence the crowd. It is not Hrothgar's own vanity that precipitates his speech but a genuine concern for the young warrior.

Hrothgar quietly begins by praising Beowulf but quickly follows with a warning. If a leader is not careful, God's gifts can lead him to vanity. The Danes' chief example of a gifted king gone wrong is Heremod, who not only failed to treat his people generously but actually killed other Danes in his own hall, a sin of unpardonable proportion in the world of the *comitatus,* the honor code binding a ruler to his thanes. Among other sins, Heremod indulged in *hubris,* an overwhelming pride or arrogance that leads to outrageous behavior. He lived a joyless life and justifiably suffered for the damage that he brought to his people.

Theme

From that example, Hrothgar generalizes about all of those who benefit from God's gifts. Only the wise and mature realize that all glory is fleeting. God will allow a "high-born heart [to] travel far in delight" (1729); one day, however, it will fall. A fool grows in his arrogance and thinks he is invincible, even forgetting that life and glory are loans from the Creator. Then Hrothgar turns to Beowulf, who has just experienced his finest victory, and warns *him* to guard against the curse of pride. Beowulf is young and strong now, but his youth and strength will not last. Defeat and death wait for him as they do for all. Hrothgar himself has ruled 50 years and seen his own glory days; but he points out that he, too, experienced failure and sorrow. Grendel's victories chased the Danes from Heorot, the great symbol of his reign, and humiliated the old king.

First joy, then sorrow. The message is repeated throughout *Beowulf.* In this harsh and often cruel world, joy never seems to last long. For this day, however, Hrothgar has finished his sermon. He directs Beowulf to return to his seat and generously signals that the feast shall continue, a second feast as impressive as the first.

The next day features generosity and departure. Beowulf returns the great sword Hrunting to Unferth. He continues to refrain from vengeance against Unferth for the earlier insults regarding the Breca contest; nor does he blame the sword for its failure in the cave fight. He is, we are told, "noble, generous in spirit" (1812), perhaps reflecting, at least for the time, virtues of Hrothgar's sermon. Beowulf generously offers to come to Hrothgar's assistance if enemies threaten the king. He speaks for his own country's ruler in welcoming Hrothgar's son to Hygelac's court if the lad chooses to visit. Hrothgar observes, prophetically, that Beowulf would make a fine king himself if the Geats should ever find themselves in need of one. He presents Beowulf with a dozen more treasures.

Hrothgar's farewell to Beowulf is poignant and sincere. Tears running down his cheeks, he embraces and kisses the young warrior as an aging father might treat a son whom he realistically does not expect to see again. Hrothgar is not a bad king. He just got old: "He was one king / blameless in everything, till age took from him / the joy of his strength—a thing that harms many" (1885–87).

Glossary

gift from the sea a reference to Grendel's head, which Beowulf brings back from the mere.

God's opponent Grendel.

race of giants here, some of the descendants of Cain.

runes letters of an alphabet used by ancient Germanic peoples, especially Scandinavians and Anglo-Saxons; sometimes cryptic.

woven snake-blade in constructing swords, numerous thin iron rods were woven together and forged to form a single blade.

Ecgwela a former Danish leader.

Heaven's hall-ruler God is metaphorically spoken of as a Germanic king.

Hrethric Hrothgar and Wealhtheow's elder son.

Hrethel father of Geats' King Hygelac; maternal grandfather of Beowulf.

gannet's bath a gannet is a large sea bird; its "bath," therefore, would be the sea itself.

Lines 1888–2199

Summary

Beowulf and his men return to their ship and set sail for Geatland. The poet interrupts his report on Beowulf's return to discuss the Geats' Queen Hygd and the qualities of a virtuous queen as contrasted to a wicked ruler like Queen Modthrytho. After this interlude, the narrator returns to Beowulf's arrival at King Hygelac's splendid hall. Hygd passes among the thanes serving mead, reminiscent of Wealhtheow's admirable hospitality at Heorot. Hygelac asks about Beowulf's journey, and the young champion recounts his visit to the Scyldings, digressing to consider Hrothgar's attempt to make peace with the Heathobards.

Returning to his own story, Beowulf briefly reports on his victory over Grendel, the surprise attack by Grendel's mother, and his triumph at the cave beneath the mere. Beowulf presents various treasures to Hygelac and Hygd, most notably presenting the queen with the magnificent gold necklace that Wealhtheow gave him. Hygelac rewards Beowulf with a rare heirloom, a sword covered with gold. He also honors the young warrior with "lands, seven thousand hides, / a hall, and gift-throne" (2195–96). Beowulf is now a lord of the realm, but it is clear that he still owes his allegiance to Hygelac.

Commentary

After Hrothgar's sermon, everything that Beowulf does must be thought of, at least in passing, within the context of the wise old king's message. As his visit to the Scyldings runs full cycle and Beowulf returns to his ship with his men, he continues to comport himself with grace and generosity. Exceeding what is expected, the Geat champion presents the Dane ship-guard with a sword so beautifully decorated in gold that the retainer will later display it proudly to his fellows at Heorot.

Modern readers may wonder why the *Beowulf* poet interrupts his narrative, just as the hero is setting foot on his homeland, to indulge in the elaborate contrast between Geatland's Queen Hygd and the murderous Queen Modthrytho. When the *scop* performed the story of Finnsburh at Heorot (1063 ff.), the interlude was a logical extension of the dramatic situation, a celebration in honor of Beowulf at which such a story might well be told. Here, the action simply stops. Beowulf has just arrived home. He is about to receive his welcome. It is a moment of some emotion and dramatic intensity. So the poet interrupts to give us a little lesson on the qualities of a proper queen. Hygd *is* a proper queen—generous, courteous and wise beyond her years. There is considerable scholarship on who she and Modthrytho might have been and why the poet makes so much of them. For our purposes, perhaps it is enough that they are simply what they appear to be—a young but effective queen who serves her king and her people well, on the one hand; and, on the other, a treacherous example of power gone wrong.

In her excessive pride and abusive treatment of subjects, Modthrytho reminds us of evil King Heremod. She even went so far as to have men executed for the offense of looking into her eyes. As beautiful and strong as she was, she was no "peace-weaver" (2017) as is Wealhtheow, for example. The poet then tells of Modthrytho's conversion through her marriage to Offa, and we get the idea that most of the *Beowulf* audience already knows this story, as it knows the rest of the poet's allusions and probably the story of Beowulf itself. Given that, the interlude may have been less of an intrusion and more of a reminder of a familiar character to the *scop*'s audience. Still, a modern reader might be forgiven if the example still seems intrusive. At any rate, the poet does finally move on to Beowulf's arrival at Hygelac's court.

Propriety is the guideline at the great hall of the Geats. Hygd, like Wealhtheow, is the perfect hostess—courteous, friendly, but courtly—as she walks among the retainers and offers mead. Hygelac formally inquires about Beowulf's trip, a venture that had concerned him because of the extreme danger involved. Beowulf is almost nonchalant in his response. He refers to the fight with Grendel as "dancing in the hall" (2003) and then interrupts his own story to consider Hrothgar's hopes for peace with the Heathobards (literally the "War-Beards"). Hrothgar has promised to give his daughter, Freawaru, to Ingeld of the Heathobards in one of those marriages designed to quell a feud. Beowulf, however, is skeptical of the outcome and imagines a scenario that causes the resumption of the old feud. In an elaborate form of dramatic irony extending beyond the current epic, *Beowulf*'s early audience almost certainly had known this story as well and that peace will not last despite the marriage. The audience thus confirms Beowulf's prescience.

Then Beowulf gives an uninspired account of his victories. The reader may wonder at the purpose of this account; even Beowulf admits that the story is "scarcely a secret to much of mankind" (2001) by the time he arrives at Hygelac's court. Although it fits dramatically, the reader should remember that the *Beowulf* epic probably was performed over the course of two or more nights. Recounting the first two victories refreshes the audience's memory and prepares it for the third major battle and the conclusion of the poem.

Theme

The theme of generosity is tied to a retainer's relationship with his king and dominates the remainder of this section. Generosity is symbolic politically and socially in Beowulf's world, significant in ways that transcend modern custom. A thane (or retainer) owes his lord first choice of treasure gained in battle. For his part, the ruler rewards the warrior with payments of gold or other values, including land, commensurate to the thane's achievements and value to his lord. Upon his return from Heorot, Beowulf reports on the Scyldings' King Hrothgar's generosity and presents Hygelac with the treasures that the young champion has earned, including "the boar's-head standard, / high-crowned helmet, great iron shirt, / [and] ornamented war-sword" (2152–2154). Hrothgar would expect the young warrior to do this.

To enhance value, Beowulf informs Hygelac of the history of the gifts. Nor does he slight Queen Hygd, honoring her with the gold necklace as well as three horses with gold saddles. This generosity demonstrates respect and loyalty. In return, Hygelac presents Beowulf with an extremely valuable gold sword that once belonged to King Hrethel; he makes Beowulf a lord, officially granting him land, his own great hall, and a "gift-throne" (2196). We are told that Hygelac and Beowulf each *inherited* land, as well, but that Hygelac is the higher in rank and head of the kingdom.

As he completes this section on Beowulf's youth, the poet seems to want to assure us that Beowulf *does* follow the tenets of Hrothgar's sermon (2177 ff.). Beowulf becomes renowned not only for his courage and strength but also for his good deeds and prudence. Never does he kill "comrades in drink" (2180), an important virtue in the *comitatus*. The brief reference to Beowulf's clumsy youth probably is left over from folk origins; there are many folk examples of inept, awkward, apparently lazy, or cowardly adolescents who grow into impressive adults.

The poet is finished with Beowulf's youth and turns to the waning years of the great man's life. As he does, the reader will do well to remember the message of Hrothgar's sermon and hope that Beowulf does, too.

Glossary

sea-wind's cloak the ship's mast.

crest-glider a kenning for *ship*.

Haereth Hygd's father.

Modthrytho an example of a disreputable ruler, possibly based on a fourth-century queen.

kinsman of Hemming here, a reference to Offa.

garrote a metal collar used for execution by strangulation or breaking the neck.

Offa king of the European (not English) Angles.

Eomer son of Offa.

Garmund Offa's father.

Ongentheow a Swedish king.

striplings adolescents, young warriors.

Ingeld a prince of the Heathobards. He will later lead a raid on Heorot and burn it before being routed.

Froda king of the Heathobards, father of Ingeld.

Withergyld a Heathobard warrior.

Hondscio literally, "hand-shoe" or glove. A Geat warrior, he was Grendel's first target the night that Beowulf killed the ogre.

chant-wood a kenning for the *scop*'s harp, with which he accompanied himself as he sang or chanted a story-song.

Heorogar brother of Hrothgar.

Heoroweard son of Heorogar.

Ecgtheow Beowulf's father.

Hrethel Hygelac's father.

Lines 2200–2400

Summary

Years pass. Hygelac is killed in battle. His son, Heardred, inherits the throne, with Beowulf's support, but is also slain. Beowulf becomes king of the Geats and rules well for 50 years. To everyone's alarm, however, a terrifying dragon begins to stalk the countryside at night, destroying homes—including Beowulf's great hall—with his fiery breath. For 300 years, the dragon has peacefully guarded a treasure-trove, originally the riches of a now-defunct tribe but long hidden in a "high barrow-hall, / towering stone-mound" (2212–13). A lone Geat fugitive, apparently a servant or slave escaping a cruel master, has stolen a single flagon from the hoard, outraging the dragon and inciting him to vengeance.

When Beowulf hears of the dragon's night raids, the king initially wonders if *he* could have angered God in some way, bringing this trouble to his people. Before long, however, the aging warrior focuses on his responsibility as protector and prepares to face the monster in battle. Although he is now an old man, Beowulf believes that he can defeat the dragon by himself. He remembers victories against Grendel and Grendel's mother, as well as a heroic escape from Frisia after Hygelac was killed. Always conscious of weapons and tactics, Beowulf prepares by ordering a new shield, made of iron, since the dragon-fire would make short sparks of his usual linden-wood. Courageous and determined, if not quite the man he once was, the old warrior sets off.

Commentary

The mutability of time is central to Hrothgar's sermon (1700–84), and it provides the framework for the final third of the poem. The passing of time brings changes to the lives of the Geats as it does to everyone. As Hrothgar warned, and as the *Beowulf* poet reminds us throughout the epic, all glory is fleeting.

Time is out of joint as the poet reveals the events leading up to Beowulf's becoming king. (For a chronology of the Geats' feuds, see Chickering, pp. 361–62.) At this point, we only know that the king and his heir have been killed in separate conflicts. Beowulf could have become king sooner but was more loyal than ambitious. Queen Hygd offered Beowulf the throne after her husband (Hygelac) died, thinking that her young son (Heardred) was unable to protect the kingdom; Beowulf refused but served the young king faithfully. After Heardred's death, Beowulf did become king and ruled his people well for 50 years. Fortunes, however, do change, as Hrothgar predicted.

The dragon is the final test for Beowulf, a test of his wisdom as well as his courage. The problem starts when a fugitive, apparently a run-away slave, stumbles across the dragon's treasure-trove. The ancient treasures in the hoard once belonged to a regional tribe of warriors; almost the entire tribe was killed in battle some 300 years previously. One sole survivor, who is called the "keeper of rings" (2244), hid the treasures in the high barrow-hall and soon died.

Style & Language

As poetry, one of the most moving passages in the epic is the Keeper's invocation as he leaves the gold and other items in the barrow (2247–2266). He speaks of the mutability of time and the loss of the good men, heroes, and princes, who no longer have any use for the treasure. They took the metals from the earth, and the Keeper now returns the treasures to it. He tells us that the stewards sleep who once burnished battle-masks. The chain-shirts can no longer protect their owners because the warriors will fight no more battles. There will be no more songs from the *scop*. The tribe's fortunes have turned. Everyone is dead. All glory is fleeting.

The dragon's motivation is vengeance even though the poet makes it clear that the fire-breathing reptile, like the deceased warriors, has no use for the cup or any of the rest of the treasure. He originally discovered the secret entrance to the barrow by chance, just as the fugitive does. Raiding at night, the dragon reminds the reader of Grendel, the monster who haunted Hrothgar in his old age and changed the Scylding king's fortunes. In a parallel that cannot be missed, the dragon does the same, in a slightly different way, to Beowulf.

Interestingly, Beowulf's initial reaction is a feeling of guilt. He believes that he has somehow offended God. However, Beowulf is nothing if not devoted to God, country, and duty. He is the protector of his people and almost immediately begins preparations to fight the dragon. Always aware of his battle gear, he orders a new shield to replace his old linden-wood protector; this one is to be covered with the strongest iron. Because Beowulf's own hall was one of the homes destroyed by the dragon, the king, too, will seek revenge.

The poet has no reservations about giving away his ending. He repeatedly tells us that Beowulf is about to meet his death. For example, in line 2311, he tells us, in the understatement of litotes, that the termination of the dragon raids will be "hard for their [the Geats'] ring-giving lord." The foreshadowing is even more specific immediately after Beowulf orders his new shield; the poet bluntly reveals that the king is "to reach the end of his seafaring days, / his life in this world, together with the serpent" (242–43).

We might question Beowulf's wisdom in deciding to fight the serpent alone, rejecting the assistance of his trained warriors. He could approach with a full army but supposedly bases his decision on former triumphs over Grendel and the mother. He also put up quite a fight when Hygelac died in Frisia; Beowulf escaped by defeating many of the enemy in close combat, carrying off the war gear of 30 men. The problem is that Beowulf was a young man during those glorious battles. At least 50 years have passed. Beowulf now is clearly an old man. Is he driven by vanity? False pride? Did not Hrothgar warn him of this in the sermon? Not just Beowulf's own life is at stake. If he dies, his people will be lost.

Glossary

Battle-Scylfings Swedes. The Geats have a long feud with the Scylfings.

Hereric Queen Hygd's brother.

swift roan Horses played an important role among the royalty, but most of the fighting was executed on foot.

dawn-scorcher, flame-snake, the worm epithets for the dragon.

Ruler's favor God's preference. Sometimes God and *wyrd* are virtually interchangeable in the poem, possibly the result of Christian substitution.

Frisia Hygelac was killed in an apparently ill-conceived battle with the western Frisians (allies of the Franks), *not* by King Finn's people of the Finnsburh episode. Hygelac's death (c. 520 AD) is one historical event in the epic; it was recorded by Saint Gregory of Tours in his *Historia Francorum*.

Hetware technically, the Chattuarii; here indistinguishable from Frisians; joined with Franks against Hygelac.

Ongentheow Scylfings' (Swedes') king killed by Hygelac's warriors Wulf and Eofor.

Ohthere and Onela Ongentheow's sons, Swedes. Onela killed Geat King Heardred.

Eadgils and Eanmund Ohthere's sons, Swedes. They had a feud with their uncle, Onela, and were temporarily sheltered by Heardred. Eadgils, supplied by Beowulf, later killed Onela.

Lines 2401–2630

Summary

With eleven of his most trusted retainers, men who have gladly accepted the gifts of a generous king, Beowulf sets out to find the dragon. Reluctantly guiding them is the fugitive who originally stole the cup from the treasure-trove. The dragon's barrow lies near the sea, between a cliff and the beach. Once there, Beowulf pauses to reflect on his life and he recalls his own glory days and the victories that he earned for his king and their people. Beowulf presents his last war speech to the select company. He will face the fire-dragon alone.

Discovering an entrance to the barrow under the stone cliff, Beowulf decides that he cannot enter due to flames already covering the passage. He calls out the dragon, and the two face off. Beowulf's new shield is less protection than he had hoped. His sword fails to penetrate the dragon's hide. Wounded and burned, the great old champion needs help. At this crucial time, all but one of his retainers abandon him, fleeing to safety in a nearby wood. Only young Wiglaf remains. Although this is his first battle, he cannot desert his king.

Commentary

It is true that the old warrior is proud; perhaps excessive pride *(ofermod)* causes him to use poor judgment, as Hrothgar warned that it might. Beowulf is up against a formidable foe, and he is no longer a young man. Employing his troops to surround the barrow and overwhelm the dragon through force of numbers might be more prudent. But Beowulf has earned the right to *try* to be a champion one more time. If his people will be considerably worse off without him—and they will—his service to them is nearly over anyway. He deserves the chance to die like a warrior.

Beowulf seems to know that he is going to die. After reaching the barrow, he sits down with his men and wishes them good fortune. The poet tells us that the old man's spirit is "sad, / restless, death-ripe" (2419–20) as he thinks back over his life. (His recollections are probably more important than the names.) Beowulf was seven years old when

King Hrethel became his foster father. Hrethel had three sons of his own: Herebeald, Haethcyn, and Hygelac. Beowulf recalls the kind generosity of the father and a tragic dilemma that is difficult for a modern audience to grasp.

The code of vengeance of the heroic age probably exceeds the modern audience's capacity to understand. When they were young men, Haethcyn killed his older brother, Herebeald, with an errant arrow in a shooting accident. Although that incident is tragic in itself, the grief was exacerbated because the code required King Hrethel to seek vengeance, even against his own son and even though the death was accidental. Unable to endure the dilemma, the father suffered and died without taking action against Haethcyn. In a passage that some critics find one of the finest examples of poetry in the epic, but which might slip by the casual reader, Beowulf compares Hrethel's grief to that of a father whose son is on the gallows (2444 ff.). The first word of the passage is correctly translated "So," but the meaning might be more clear if it were "So also" or "Thus." Haethcyn is not the one on the gallows. Succeeding his father as king, *he* is killed in the feud with the Swedes (Scylfings). The crown then went to the third brother, Hygelac.

The poet once more has interrupted the dramatic flow, but this time the interruption is effective. In addition to the losses in his foster family, Beowulf recalls many personal victories. He is proud that he served Hygelac well and, like any old man reflecting on his youth, delights in his glories. He always *led* the troops into battle and is not about to back off now.

Addressing his men for the last time, Beowulf seems apologetic about using *weapons* against the dragon. He says he would fight barehanded, as he did against Grendel, if he knew a way to do so against this enemy. At any rate, he promises not to retreat. How ironic and sad that Beowulf thinks he needs to explain any of his actions or decisions to men who will flee in fear when the battle commences.

The old champion certainly does not lack courage as he calls out the dragon, his voice "a strong-hearted bellow" (2552) one last time. This is no place for more talk; it is a battleground. The earth shakes as the two meet, the dragon clearly gaining early advantage as Beowulf's shield provides little protection, and his sword chips against the hide of the reptile, reminiscent of the failure of Hrunting against Grendel's mother. For the first time, Beowulf feels that he will lose a fight and be forced to "give up loaned time" (2590) on earth. The great champion is injured and needs help. Violating all concepts of the heroic code, ten of his men flee for the safety of the nearby woods. Only Wiglaf remains. After the poet offers a brief introduction of the young retainer and his battle gear, we are ready for the final showdown.

Glossary

Hrethel king of the Geats, son of Swerting.

Herebeald, Haethcyn, and Hygelac sons of Hrethel, in order of seniority.

Sorrow Hill in Geatland, site of a battle where Swedes ambushed the Geats after Hrethel's death.

Haethcyn killed in battle at Ravenswood (in Sweden) by Ongentheow while avenging battle of Sorrow Hill. Hygelac immediately took over leadership of the Geats.

Ongentheow Swede king, father of Onela and Ohthere; killed by Hygelac's retainers Wulf and Eofor at Ravenswood.

Gifthas eastern Germanic tribe.

Daeghrefn a Frisian warrior, champion of the Hugas, whose beating heart Beowulf, as a young man, crushed with his bare hands.

Hugas a Frisian subgroup or family.

his heirloom sword Beowulf's sword in the dragon fight is called "Naegling."

Weohstan probably part Swede (Scylfing) and part Geat (as Chickering suggests, p. 369), father of Wiglaf. Weohstan apparently killed the Swede Eanmund on behalf of the victim's uncle, Onela, and was rewarded with Eanmund's war gear, which he eventually passed on to Wiglaf.

Aelfhere Some scholars think that this is a reference to Beowulf, indicating that Wiglaf is related, perhaps a cousin.

Waegmunding scholars dispute whether this clan, with which Wiglaf and Beowulf are associated, is Swede or Geat or a mixture of the two.

Lines 2631–2820

Summary

Wiglaf calls to the other ten retainers and reminds them of the promises that they made to Beowulf. In exchange for his protection and gifts, they all had vowed to fight for their king whenever he needed them. Even though Beowulf intended to deal with the dragon one-on-one, he now clearly needs help. The other thanes do not return.

Although he realizes that he may die in the battle, Wiglaf rushes to Beowulf's defense. Wiglaf's wooden shield burns as the dragon attacks again. The young retainer ducks behind Beowulf's iron shield, which is no great help but is better than nothing. Beowulf musters the strength to swing his mighty sword, Naegling, one last time; unfortunately, it snaps on the dragon's head. The dragon charges again, piercing Beowulf's neck with his sharp fangs. Although his hand is sorely burned, Wiglaf finds a vulnerable spot well beneath the dragon's head and thrusts his sword into the monster. The dragon's fire decreases. Beowulf rallies to use his knife and is able to cut into the monster's entrails, killing him. Realizing he is dying, Beowulf speaks his final words as Wiglaf attempts to comfort him.

Commentary

Wiglaf's speech is an attempt to remind the other ten retainers of the honor code of *comitatus* and to shame them into action. In this system, a lord or king offers protection to his retainers (or thanes) and supports them with a share of booty, gifts, and even land. In exchange, the retainers pledge loyalty to the death on behalf of the ruler. Specifically, Wiglaf recalls a time when he and the ten other warriors received rings and the very armor that they now have with them from Beowulf. Consistent with the heroic code, they promised to come to his assistance if he ever needed them. Wiglaf rightly accuses them of running when they vowed to fight. He declares that he would rather be burned to death than to abandon his king, and he rushes to Beowulf's assistance.

The final battle features the kind of staccato interchange that the *Beowulf* poet depicts so well. The action here (2669–2708) is tight, detailed, and furious, some of the best in the poem. Wiglaf rushes to Beowulf's side. The dragon almost immediately reduces the young retainer's shield to cinders. As Wiglaf ducks behind Beowulf's shield, the old warrior summons the strength to swing his famous sword so hard that it snaps against the dragon's head. Seeing his chance, the dragon charges once more, seizing Beowulf by the neck with his poisonous fangs. Distressed by his king's situation, Wiglaf throws all care aside and attacks, even though his fighting hand is seriously burned in the process. He finds an unprotected spot and thrusts his sword into the dragon, cutting off the source of the monster's fire-breath. Beowulf manages one last blow, a thrust with his knife that opens the dragon's belly and kills the mighty beast. Beowulf is poisoned from the dragon's fangs and bleeding badly.

The bond between the dying mentor and his protégé is apparent as Beowulf speaks to the young man and Wiglaf tries to comfort him. They have literally shared a baptism of fire, the only kind of character test that Beowulf trusts. Although Wiglaf is not his offspring, Beowulf thinks of him as a son when the king, unable to stand, briefly reflects on his life and passes control of the Geats to the brave young retainer. Beowulf makes clear that *he* has been a good king, not at all like Heremod, the disreputable example in Hrothgar's sermon. The old man has protected his people well; no one dared to attack the Geats for 50 years. He has accepted what the years offered and never murdered his own, direct references to the sermon. Finally, he has given his life for the treasure that, he thinks, will go to his people. (Ironically, the treasure will be buried with Beowulf and will be of no more use to the Geats than it was to the dragon.) Beowulf wants to see some of the riches. Hoping to please his king, Wiglaf leaves for a moment and enters the barrow.

The scene inside is reminiscent of the ogres' cave after Beowulf killed Grendel's mother. Both hold impressive treasure that will come to no use. Wiglaf sees wonderful tapestry, jewels, gold in various forms, and a golden standard hanging over the riches, emitting a strange light like that in the cave. Wiglaf brings some of the treasure to his leader who is near death.

Beowulf's final words (2794 ff.) are a mixture of prayer, instruction, and farewell. Thanking God, he tells Wiglaf that he wants his ashes buried in a mound on Whale's Cliff (*Hrones-naesse*) near the sea where passing sailors might look upon it and call it "Beowulf's Barrow" (*Biowulfes biorh*). The dying king then symbolically passes his position on to Wiglaf by giving the young man the armor, rings, and gold collar that Beowulf is wearing. Wiglaf is the last of the Waegmundings, Beowulf's clan, but he has *earned* the right to rule, not inherited it. In a poignant passage, the dying king says that "fate has swept / all my kinsmen to their final doom" (2814–15). He must follow his ancestors. Having spoken his last, Beowulf "chose / the high battle-flames; out from his breast / his soul went to seek the doom of the just" (2818–20).

Glossary

high battle flames a funeral pyre suitable for a great warrior.

doom here, eternal judgment.

Lines 2821–3182

Summary

Grieving over the death of Beowulf, the man who was "dearest in his life" (2822), Wiglaf bends over the corpse, gently washing his king as if hoping to restore him. The other ten retainers come out of the woods and receive a harsh lecture from their new king. Wiglaf sends a messenger to speak to other Geats who are not far away, waiting for news of the battle. The messenger reports Beowulf's death. Anticipating renewed problems with the Swedes, he recounts the history of their feud with the Geats. Sadly Wiglaf calls the company to visit Beowulf's death site where they can see the huge ("fifty foot-paces" long, 3042) body of the dragon as well as Beowulf's corpse.

Wiglaf speaks to the assembled Geats, informing them of the old king's funeral directions and setting them to work on the pyre at Whale's Cliff. With seven thanes, the new leader hauls the treasure out of the barrow. The audience learns that the cache had been cursed and is to be buried with Beowulf. The funeral pyre is immense; the grief of the old king's people is profound. One nameless woman sings a lament for the fallen hero, expressing terror at the future of the Geats without his protection. Constructing the funeral barrow takes 10 days. In it are placed Beowulf's ashes and the treasure for which he died. It is said that they lie there even now.

Commentary

Wiglaf's devotion to his king is most touchingly illustrated in the scene in which the young retainer tends to the corpse. Within the limits of the manuscript, it is fair to picture the young warrior kneeling, holding the lifeless body, not washing it in preparation for a funeral but hoping to give comfort to the man "dearest in his life" (2822), now beyond human comfort. We can hear the anger in Wiglaf's voice as he reprimands the 10 cowards who fled to the woods when their master needed them most.

Theme

Counting the thief, there were 12 with Beowulf that day, and we can understand those who find parallels with Jesus Christ and his disciples. As tempting as that interpretation may be, this scene is really about the heroic code of the *comitatus,* the relationship between ruler and followers that provides order and structure to the civilization of the Geats. Wiglaf begins slowly, almost calmly, but his contempt for the 10 and love for his king lead him into a long, convoluted first sentence that is fierce with retribution before its end (2864–71). These were Beowulf's own thanes, his most trusted men, supposedly loyal warriors, and they *betrayed* their king completely. Wiglaf is proud of his own attempt "beyond my strength, to help my kinsman" (2879) when his liege needed him most. As the new king, he condemns the 10 and all their kin to exile, disowning them and denying their future rights to property, wealth, or membership in the *comitatus*, stating that it is better to die than to live in shame, a maxim that Beowulf would and did support.

The messenger sent to report the results of the battle warns the people that the king's death probably will encourage old enemies to renew their feuds with the Geats. This is another example of the *Beowulf* poet interrupting the flow of the action to allude to other stories in a way that may seem odd to a modern audience. We can only conclude that *his* audience must have welcomed the allusions; these are details with which most of them were familiar. For the modern reader, however, the point could been made more simply: The king is dead. The Geats are in trouble. But that is a story for another time.

The curse on the treasure-trove seems to come from a mixture of sources. While the concept seems pagan, the poet insists on saying that "the Lord" (3054) controlled the spell and that only He could decide who might disturb the hoard. The poet makes a reference to the treasure's being "in the deeps of the earth for a thousand years" (3050), which sounds biblical (Chickering suggests Revelations 20: 7–8) but certainly doesn't match the 300 years that, we've been told, have passed since the hoard was buried. It is unclear whether Beowulf was killed because of the curse.

Always capable of surprising us, the poet turns from these digressions to one of the most beautiful extended passages in the poem, the description of the funeral pyre and the final resting place of the ashes of the great man. At Beowulf's request, the pyre is hung with battle gear. The king himself is placed respectfully at the top in the center. The flame itself is spoken of as if it is perhaps a warrior called to a ceremonial death dance: "[T]he great fire was wakened. The wood-smoke climbed up, / black above flames; the roaring one danced, / encircled by wailing . . . " (3144–46).

Several critics point out that the final lines of the poem might serve as Beowulf's epitaph:

> They said that he was, of the kings in this world,
>
> the kindest to his men, the most courteous man,
>
> the best to his people, and most eager for fame (3180–82).

That the closing does not speak of Beowulf's courage or strength or victories in battle is interesting. What it says of Beowulf is that he was kind. He knew decorum. He was good to his people. He was, in short, the exemplar of a civilized king. Some people are bothered by the last words of the poem: "most eager for fame" *(lof-geornost)*. They seem to think that "fame" is a superficial goal. We might understand better if we remember that "fame" is really *reputation* for Beowulf. To him, his reputation was everything.

Glossary

Franks and Frisians Germanic tribes united in opposition to the Geats.

Hugas a Frisian subgroup or family.

Hetware joined with the Franks against Hygelac.

Merovingian pertaining to the Franks.

Ravenswood site (in Sweden) of major battle between Geats and Swedes.

swathe to wrap with bandages.

Eofor and Wulf fought Swedes' King Ongentheow to his death. For a chronology of the Geats' feuds, see Chickering, pp. 361–62.

CHARACTER ANALYSES

The following critical analyses delve into the physical, emotional, and psychological traits of the literary work's major characters so that you might better understand what motivates these characters. The writer of this study guide provides this scholarship as an educational tool by which you may compare your own interpretations of the characters. Before reading the character analyses that follow, consider first writing your own short essays on the characters as an exercise by which you can test your understanding of the original literary work. Then, compare your essays to those that follow, noting discrepancies between the two. If your essays appear lacking, that might indicate that you need to re-read the original literary work or re-familiarize yourself with the major characters.

Beowulf

The reader is first introduced to Beowulf as he disembarks from his ship, having just arrived in the land of the Danes (Scyldings) from his home in Geatland. He is an impressive-looking man. The Scylding coastal guard points out that he has never seen "a mightier noble, / a larger man" (247–48) even though he has held this office and served his king, Hrothgar, for many years, watching all kinds of warriors come and go. Beowulf is huge and strong. We are soon told that he has the strength of 30 men in his hand-grip. Just as important is the way that the young warrior (not much more than 20 years of age) carries himself; the Geat has the bearing of a noble leader, a champion, perhaps a prince. He has arrived to help the Scyldings; for 12 years, a mighty man-like ogre named Grendel has menaced Hrothgar's great mead-hall, Heorot, terrorizing and devouring the Danes.

In a seminal lecture, often anthologized (see CliffsNotes Resource Center), English novelist and scholar J. R. R. Tolkien (*"Beowulf*: The Monsters and the Critics," *Proceedings of the British Academy,* XXII [1936], 245–95) argues that the central structural motif of *Beowulf* is the balance between beginnings and endings, of youth and age. The most dominating example of this is the life of Beowulf himself. When he arrives in Hrothgar's kingdom, the hero of the epic is still a very young man. He is out to establish a name for himself. Reputation is a key theme of the poem and of central importance to Beowulf. As the coastal guard first approaches the Geats, he asks about Beowulf's lineage (251). Beowulf mentions his father's accomplishments and reputation as well as his king, Hygelac, and his people, the Geats. To King Hrothgar (418 ff.), he properly reveals more: Beowulf once killed a tribe of giants and has driven enemies from his homeland. He already has a favorable reputation, but he is eager for more achievements that will add to his good name. In the world of *Beowulf,* a man's good name is his key to immortality. It is all that remains after death.

Part of the motivation for the hero's coming to the land of the Danes is to gain more *fame.* The poem uses the word unabashedly, but a modern audience might feel uncomfortable with the concept, thinking of empty trophies in a superficial frame. Within this world of heroic struggle, however, fame is more than that. A modern audience might best think of fame as *reputation.* Reputation can protect a leader's people and settle a conflict before it comes to blows, as Beowulf's reputation later does when he is the king of Geatland. Fame is a positive quality, having to do more with earned respect than vanity.

A more important reason for coming to Hrothgar's aid is directly related to a family debt. Years before, Hrothgar sheltered Beowulf's father, Ecgtheow, from a dangerous feud and purchased a settlement of the conflict with the Geat's enemies, a procedure incorporating *wergild* (man-payment or man-worth). Beowulf has come to repay Hrothgar's generosity.

At a banquet in the Geats' honor on the first day of their visit, a drunken, jealous Dane named Unferth challenges Beowulf's reputation. When Beowulf was an adolescent, he engaged in a swimming match on the open sea with another boy, a royal member of the Brondings tribe named Breca. Unferth asserts that Beowulf was vain and foolish to enter such a dangerous contest and that Breca proved the stronger, defeating Beowulf in seven nights. Unferth's point is that, if the Geat could not win that swimming match, he is surely no match for Grendel.

Beowulf's response to Unferth (529 ff.) further establishes the hero's character and maturity. He remains composed and in control, despite his youth. Although he would be justified in calling Unferth out and attacking him physically, Beowulf instead uses wit and facts to correct the Dane. He begins by observing, "What a great deal, Unferth my friend, / full of beer, you have said about Breca, / told of his deeds" (530–32). Beowulf points out that he and Breca swam for five nights, not seven. Although he was the stronger, he would not abandon Breca. After rough seas drove them apart, Beowulf spent the rest of the fifth night fighting vicious water monsters, killing nine. He comments on the workings of Fate *(Wyrd),* saying that it saved him but only because it was not his time and because he had fought courageously. Beowulf reminds the gathering that Unferth's reputation is sparse except for the fact that he actually killed his own brothers, for which he will be condemned to hell even though he may be "clever" with words. Beowulf also points out that Grendel might not be such a problem for King Hrothgar if Unferth's "battle-spirit, were as sharp as [his] words" (596). The rebuttal is an enormous success; before he ever faces Grendel, Beowulf proves that he is a man to be reckoned with.

The confrontation with Grendel clearly demonstrates Beowulf's great strength, but it also illustrates his sense of fair play and his cool reasoning regarding tactics. Beowulf refuses to wear armor or use weapons against the ogre because Grendel is not schooled in the fine art of human warfare and will use no weapons himself. Ironically, the choice to eschew weapons ends up helping Beowulf because Grendel is protected from them by a magic charm. To defeat him, an opponent *must* be superior in hand-to-claw combat. To study the ogre's approach, Beowulf allows Grendel to attack and devour another of the Geats when the descendant of Cain enters Heorot that night. Although he is losing a friend, Beowulf observes but lies still. When the ogre reaches for his next victim, he receives the shock of his life. Beowulf, with the hand-grip of 30 men, grabs hold and won't let go. The ensuing battle nearly destroys Heorot but ends with a victory for Beowulf. He rips Grendel's right claw from its shoulder socket, mortally wounding the beast and sending him scurrying in retreat. The claw hangs from Heorot's roof, a macabre trophy.

Beowulf's defeat of Grendel's mother demonstrates remarkable courage and perseverance. Seeking to avenge the death of her son and recover his claw, the mother attacks Heorot the next night, surprising everyone. In the morning, Beowulf tracks her to a dark, swampy mere where she and her son live in a cave at the bottom of the lake. There Beowulf defeats her with the help of a magic giant sword and returns with the sword's hilt and Grendel's head as trophies. In a sermon designed to guide Beowulf through a life of leadership, King Hrothgar warns the young warrior of the dangers of pride and the perils of old age.

Beowulf's reputation spreads in the last third of the poem. He serves his king well until Hygelac is killed in battle. When Hygelac's son dies in a feud, Beowulf becomes king and rules successfully for 50 years. Like Hrothgar, however, his peace in his declining years is shattered by a menacing monster. The question at the end of Beowulf's life is whether he allows pride to blind him from prudent action. Does he love fame too much?

A fiery dragon terrorizes the countryside because a lone Geat fugitive has stolen a golden flagon from the dragon's treasure-trove. Beowulf insists on fighting the dragon alone even though the king's death will leave Geatland vulnerable to attack from old enemies. Led by the fugitive and accompanied by eleven of his warriors, Beowulf seeks out the dragon's barrow. Beowulf's trusted sword, Naegling, is no match for the monster. Seeing his king in trouble, one thane, Wiglaf, goes to his assistance while the others flee to the woods. Together, Wiglaf and Beowulf kill the dragon, but the mighty king is mortally wounded. He has won every battle but one. Some critics feel that, despite the warnings by Hrothgar, pride and age have brought down the epic hero. Others point out that Beowulf did not have long to rule anyway and deserved the right to choose a warrior's death.

Wiglaf

The one retainer who comes to Beowulf's aid in the battle against the dragon represents the theme of loyalty in the system of the *comitatus*. This is the honor code that exists between the king, or feudal lord, and his warriors, sometimes called "thanes" or "retainers." (Technically, retainers would be of higher rank, but the words are often used interchangeably.) Thanes swear devotion to their leader and vow to fight boldly, to the death if necessary, for him. For his part, the leader rewards his thanes with treasure, protection, and land. His generosity is one of the virtues for which he is admired.

Wiglaf is a young warrior in the service of his king, Beowulf. We are told that he is a kinsman of Beowulf, the last of the Waegmunding clan. When he realizes that Beowulf is in serious jeopardy in his battle with the dragon, Wiglaf calls to the other 10 retainers who accompanied the king to the barrow and reminds them of the promises they have made to their leader. He recalls a time when he and the other ten received rings and the very armor that they now have with them from Beowulf. Consistent with the heroic code, they promised to come to the assistance of their king if he ever needed them. Wiglaf rightly accuses them of running when they vowed to fight. He attempts to shame them into action, but no one returns. Wiglaf is the only one willing to risk his life to help his ruler. He declares that he would rather be burned to death than to abandon his king, and he rushes to Beowulf's defense.

It is Wiglaf's blow that slows the serpent and decreases his firepower, thus enabling Beowulf to manage one last thrust with a knife that opens the dragon's belly and kills him.

The bond between Beowulf and Wiglaf is apparent as the king speaks to the young man and Wiglaf tries to comfort him. They have literally shared a baptism of fire, the test of battle that is the only criterion earning Beowulf's trust. Although Wiglaf is not his offspring, Beowulf thinks of him as a son when the dying king, unable to stand, briefly reflects on his life and passes control of Geatland on to the brave young retainer. Wiglaf has *earned* the right to rule, not inherited it. If he is not as mighty as his heroic predecessor, he certainly lacks nothing in courage and loyalty.

Grendel

The ogre who has menaced Hrothgar's people for 12 years is a huge, powerful descendant of the biblical Cain, the son of Adam and Eve, who killed his brother Abel out of jealousy (Genesis 4). Cain's name in Hebrew is *Qayin,* meaning "creature," and, according to legend, the monsters of the earth are his descendants. Grendel is envious, resentful, and angry *toward mankind,* possibly because he feels that God blesses them but that the ogre himself never can be blessed. Grendel especially resents the light, joy, and music that he observes in Hrothgar's beautiful mead-hall, Heorot. The *scop*'s "Song of Creation" (90–98) especially enrages him because it tells of the beauty and light of God's creation.

Although Grendel looks something like a man—having two arms (or claws), two legs, and one head—he is much larger and can defeat dozens of men at a time. He is protected from man's weapons by a magic charm. He devours some of the dead on the spot and carries others back to his lair, the cave he shares with his mother beneath a mere in a dark fen. The first night that Beowulf is with the Scyldings, Grendel stomps up from the swamp, bashes open the mead-hall's door with a single tap, and quickly wolfs down one of the Geats inside.

The passage describing Grendel's ascent from the fen (710–727) is one of the finest in Anglo-Saxon poetry. The drama increases as the poet describes Grendel's approach in set stages. Dark skies contrast with "the shining wine-hall" (715), a source of joy to men and the symbol of civilization. Grendel has ruled the hall for 12 years, often spending his nights there as the Danes hid elsewhere. He expects to rule again this night but meets a human warrior equal to the ogre's strength and superior in his tactics.

Beowulf observes the monster's method as one Geat is slaughtered and devoured. Grendel has no chance after that. Although the battle is furious, Beowulf has won as soon as he is able to grasp his enemy's claw. The ogre is vulnerable because Beowulf uses no weapons, and the hero has the strength of 30 men in his grip. Beowulf rips the monster's arm from its shoulder. Mortally wounded, Grendel flees to the swamp. The giant claw later hangs from Heorot's roof as a trophy.

In many ways, Grendel is the most interesting character in the epic. He is a mix of man and beast; his fury is based on very human feelings of resentment and jealousy. The novelist and Anglo-Saxon scholar John Gardner explores the inner conflicts of the character in his 1971 novel, *Grendel,* an intensely moving, funny, and perceptive book.

Grendel's Mother

Grendel's mother (sometimes called his "dam") is not as huge or as powerful as the son, but she is motivated by revenge. Her son has returned to their cave mortally wounded, one of his two arms (or claws) ripped from its shoulder socket and hanging, now, beneath the roof of Hrothgar's mead-hall. Instead of cowering in grief, the mother seeks revenge.

Although the Danes have *heard* that the swamp may harbor two ogres, they seem to believe that the problem is solved when Beowulf defeats Grendel. On the night after that victory, the Scyldings celebrate with a great deal of food and drink. Many of the celebrants spend that night in Heorot while Beowulf sleeps elsewhere. The mother stalks up from her mere, retrieving her son's claw and murderously abducting one of the Scyldings from the mead-hall.

When Beowulf comes after her, the mother has another advantage. She is in her home territory, which she has ruled for a hundred years. As the Geat champion dives deep into the lake, the mother waits and attacks only when he nears the bottom. He is virtually helpless as she drags him to the dry, eerily lighted cave for the kill. Once on dry land, however, Beowulf is able to mount a counter-attack. Although his sword, Hrunting, loaned to him by Unferth, fails to penetrate the mother's hide, Beowulf discovers a giant magic sword in the cave and is able to kill the mother with it. The sword melts to its hilt after Beowulf uses it to decapitate the corpse of Grendel, which lies nearby. He returns to Heorot with a greater trophy, the head of the ogre, as well as the hilt of the magic sword.

Some critics feel that Grendel's mother receives inadequate consideration in the poem. Her motive is as human as it is monstrous as she seeks revenge for her defeated son and reclaims his arm, which from her point of view must seem a barbaric trophy. She has lived in the mere for a hundred years and was never the problem that her son was. Nevertheless, this is Beowulf's poem; the mother is just another monster in a heroic epic. Other writers will have to enhance her tale.

Hrothgar

The king of the Danes (Scyldings) is a wise and great man, but he has lost some of his strength with age. In his prime, Hrothgar built the Scyldings into a powerful military and social entity, symbolized by the erection of his great mead-hall, Heorot. More a palace, Heorot is decorated with gold and fine tapestries. It is the center of Hrothgar's kingdom and a place of joy and light, which is exactly what Grendel, who has been raiding the hall for a dozen years, resents. For some time, Hrothgar's men have spent their nights elsewhere as Grendel freely bivouacs in Heorot.

Hrothgar has become famous for his leadership and generosity, important virtues that are closely linked in the world of *Beowulf*. As a young king, he once protected Beowulf's now deceased father, Ecgtheow, during a blood feud and purchased peace with Ecgtheow's enemies through a kind of payment known as *wergild*, providing major reasons for Beowulf's devotion to Hrothgar at the beginning of the poem. Hrothgar also became famous for taking care of his own thanes, sharing treasure and land with them as the heroic code of *comitatus* prescribes.

Hrothgar's speech to Beowulf (1700 ff.) before the Geats depart, known as "Hrothgar's Sermon," is important thematically as it warns of the dangers of fame and the mutability of time. Hrothgar speaks of the temptations of *hubris* (excessive pride) and tells young Beowulf always to remember that great joy is followed by great sorrow. The old king offers his own life as an example of the changing fortunes that can come with age. Foreshadowing Beowulf's trials in later life, Hrothgar points out that *he* ruled successfully for 50 years until Grendel brought him to his knees. Beowulf, whom Hrothgar thinks of as a son, must beware of pride and old age. Throughout the last third of the poem, we are haunted by Hrothgar's message and compelled to view Beowulf's actions in the context of the sermon.

Unferth

Along with Grendel, Unferth represents the theme of envy in the epic. Shortly after Beowulf's arrival, Unferth, full of mead, insults the guest at a banquet. This is more than an awkward moment for the hosts. Unferth's behavior goes against the code of hospitality. Unferth accuses Beowulf, as a lad, of entering a dangerous, foolish seven-night swimming match on the open sea against a boy named Breca—and losing.

Fortunately for the Dane, Beowulf demonstrates a noble spirit as well as ease with language as he refutes the charge and puts Unferth in his place. In fact, Beowulf says, he swam with Breca for five nights, not wanting to abandon the weaker boy. Rough seas separated them, and Beowulf had to kill nine mighty sea monsters before going ashore the next day. Beowulf points out that Unferth's fame lies mainly in the fact that he killed his own brothers. If the Dane could fight as well as he talks, says Beowulf, King Hrothgar might not have such a problem with Grendel.

Unferth later admits Beowulf's superiority after the defeat of Grendel and lends him a treasured sword, Hrunting, for the battle with Grendel's mother. While the sword is ineffective, at least the Dane is making an effort. We might suspect that Unferth's character flaws will surface again, but he has been humbled and his character improved for the purposes of this story.

Wealhtheow

Hrothgar's queen is an embodiment of hospitality and good taste as she hosts the banquets in Heorot. She is everything that a queen should be: generous, tasteful, proper, and kind. Her graceful appearance shortly after the Unferth incident contrasts effectively with the rude behavior of the drunken retainer. Wealhtheow is a peace-weaver and takes an active role in diplomacy, generously presenting Beowulf with a valuable gold collar and asking him to serve as counselor to her sons.

The role of women, who were still thought of as their husbands' possessions, is limited in *Beowulf*. Sometimes they were used as peacemakers between feuding tribes who found uniting through marriage to be in their best interests. The poet indicates that Wealhtheow came to Hrothgar as a result of that kind of union.

CRITICAL ESSAYS

On the pages that follow, the writer of this study guide provides critical scholarship on various aspects of Beowulf. These interpretive essays are intended solely to enhance your understanding of the original literary work; they are supplemental materials and are not to replace your reading of Beowulf. When you're finished reading Beowulf, and prior to your reading this study guide's critical essays, consider making a bulleted list of what you think are the most important themes and symbols. Write a short paragraph under each bullet explaining why you think that theme or symbol is important; include at least one short quote from the original literary work that supports your contention. Then, test your list and reasons against those found in the following essays. Do you include themes and symbols that the study guide author doesn't? If so, this self test might indicate that you are well on your way to understanding original literary work. But if not, perhaps you will need to re-read Beowulf.

Major Themes

A theme in a literary work is a recurring, unifying subject or idea, a motif that allows us to understand more deeply the character and their world. In Beowulf, the major themes reflect the values and the motivations of the characters.

Loyalty

One of the central themes of *Beowulf,* embodied by its title character, is loyalty. At every step of his career, loyalty is Beowulf's guiding virtue.

Beowulf comes to the assistance of the Danes (Scyldings) for complicated reasons. Certainly he is interested in increasing his reputation and gaining honor and payment for his own king back in Geatland. However, we soon learn that a major motivation is a family debt that Beowulf owes to Hrothgar. The young Geat is devoted to the old king because Hrothgar came to the assistance of Beowulf's father, Ecgtheow, years before. Now deceased, Ecgtheow had killed a leader of another tribe in a blood feud. When the tribe sought vengeance, Hrothgar, then a young king, sheltered Beowulf's father and settled the feud by paying tribute *(wergild)* in the form of "fine old treasures" (472) to Ecgtheow's enemies. Hrothgar even remembers Beowulf as a child. The tie between the families goes back many years, and Beowulf is proud to be able to lend his loyal services to Hrothgar.

When the hero returns to Geatland, he continues his loyalty to his uncle and king, Hygelac, risking his life even when the tactics of the ruler are not the best. After Hygelac is killed in an ill-advised raid on Frisia, Beowulf makes a heroic escape (2359 ff.) back to Geatland. Beowulf could become king then but is more loyal than ambitious. Queen Hygd offers Beowulf the throne after her husband dies, thinking that her young son (Heardred) is unable to protect the kingdom; Beowulf refuses and serves the young king faithfully. After Heardred is killed, Beowulf does become king and rules with honor and fidelity to his office and his people for 50 years. In his final test, the burden of loyalty will rest on other, younger shoulders.

Preparing for his last battle, with the fiery dragon, Beowulf puts his trust in 11 of his finest men, retainers who have vowed to fight to the death for him. Although the now elderly king insists on taking on the dragon alone, he brings along the 11 in case he needs them. When it is apparent that Beowulf is losing the battle to the dragon, however, all

but one of his men run and hide in the woods. Only Wiglaf, an inex-
perienced thane who has great respect for his king, remains loyal. Wiglaf
calls to the others in vain. Realizing that they will be no help and that
his king is about to be killed, he stands beside the old man to fight to
the death—theirs or the dragon's. For Beowulf, sadly, it is the end.
Although he and Wiglaf kill the dragon, the king dies. As he dies,
Beowulf passes the kingdom on to the brave and loyal Wiglaf.

Reputation

Another motivating factor for Beowulf—and a central theme in the
epic—is reputation. From the beginning, Beowulf is rightly concerned
about how the rest of the world will see him. He introduces himself to
the Scyldings by citing achievements that gained honor for him and his
king. When a drunken Unferth verbally assaults Beowulf at the first
banquet, at issue is the hero's reputation. Unferth's slur is the worst kind
of insult for Beowulf because his reputation is his most valuable pos-
session. Reputation is also the single quality that endures after death,
his one key to immortality. That's why Beowulf later leaves the gold in
the cave beneath the mere, after defeating the mother, preferring to
return with Grendel's head and the magic sword's hilt rather than treasure. He has and continues to amass treasures; his intent now is in building his fame.

Unferth's slur accuses Beowulf of foolishly engaging in a seven-day
swimming contest on the open sea, as a youth, and losing. If Beowulf
can't win a match like that, Unferth asserts, he surely can't defeat Grendel. Beowulf defends his reputation with such grace and persuasion that
he wins the confidence of King Hrothgar and the rest of the Danes. He
points out that he swam with Breca for *five* nights, not wanting to abandon the weaker boy. Rough seas then drove them apart, and Beowulf
had to kill nine sea monsters before going ashore in the morning. His
reputation intact, Beowulf prepares to meet Grendel and further
enhance his fame.

As he discusses Beowulf's later years, the poet lists the virtues (2177
ff.) leading to the great man's fine reputation. Beowulf is courageous
and famous for his performance in battle but equally well known for
his good deeds. Although aggressive in war, Beowulf has "no savage
mind" (2180) and never kills his comrades when drinking, an important quality in the heroic world of the mead-hall. Beowulf respects the
gifts of strength and leadership that he possesses.

As he prepares to meet the dragon, near the end of the poem, now King Beowulf again considers his reputation. He insists on facing the dragon alone despite the fact that his death will leave his people in jeopardy. Hrothgar's Sermon warned Beowulf of the dangers of pride, and some critics have accused the great warrior of excessive pride *(hubris)* in the defense of his reputation. A more considerate judgment might be that Beowulf is an old man with little time left and deserves the right to die as a warrior. The final words of the poem, stating that Beowulf was "most eager for fame" (3182), might be best understood by a modern audience by remembering that, in Beowulf's world, fame is synonymous with reputation.

Generosity and Hospitality

The Scyldings' King Hrothgar and Queen Wealhtheow embody the themes of generosity and hospitality. The code of the *comitatus* is at the heart of the *Beowulf* epic. In this system, the king or feudal lord provides land, weapons, and a share of treasure to his warriors (called thanes or retainers) in return for their support of the leader in battle. The leader's generosity is one of his highest qualities. There are more than 30 different terms for "king" in the poem, and many of them have to do with this role as provider. He is the "ring-giver" (35) or the "treasure-giver" (607); his seat of power is the "gift-throne" (168).

When booty is seized from an enemy in battle, everything goes to the king. He then allots treasure to each warrior according to the man's achievements as a soldier. When Beowulf defeats Grendel and Grendel's mother, he expects and receives great riches as his reward, including a golden banner, helmet, and mail-shirt, as well as a jeweled sword, magnificent horses with golden trappings that hang to the ground, a gem-studded saddle, and a golden collar. Such generosity is emblematic of Hrothgar's character. In turn, Beowulf will present these treasures to his own king, Hygelac, who will then honor Beowulf with appropriate gifts. Propriety/generosity is, thus, a crucial part of the political, military, social, and economic structure of the culture.

Wealhtheow shares in the gift giving and is the perfect hostess. When she serves mead in Heorot, it is an act of propriety and diplomacy, attending first to her king and then to various guests, paying special attention to Beowulf. An improper queen would be one like Modthrytho (1931 ff.) who was so inhospitable as to have her own warriors executed for the offense of merely looking into her eyes.

Hospitality is such an established part of the culture that the poet feels free to refer to it with casual humor. When Beowulf reports to Hrothgar on his victory over Grendel (957 ff.), he ironically speaks in terms of hospitality. He tried, he says, to "welcome my enemy" (969) with a firm handshake but was disappointed when he received only a "visitor's token" (971), Grendel's giant claw, "that dear [meaning 'precious'] gift" (973), a kind of macabre gratuity for services rendered. Beowulf had, ironically speaking, tried to be the perfect host; but he wanted the entire ogre body as his *tip*. Grendel left only his claw as a cheap compensation.

Envy

Despite Unferth's jealous rant at the first banquet, the most serious embodiment of envy in the poem is Grendel. The ogre who has menaced Hrothgar's people for 12 years is envious of the Danes because he can never share in mankind's hope or joy. The monster's motivation is one of the few undeniably Christian influences in the epic. Grendel is a descendant of Cain, the biblical son of Adam and Eve who killed his brother Abel out of jealousy (Genesis 4). The legend is that the monsters of the earth are Cain's descendants and eternally damned. Grendel resents men because God blesses them but will never bless him. The bright lights and sounds of joy emanating from Hrothgar's magnificent mead-hall, Heorot, especially annoy the ogre.

The *scop*'s "Song of Creation" angers Grendel because it reminds him of the light and hope of God's creation and the loss he suffers because of Cain's sin. Grendel stomps up from the mere to devour Danes and rule nightly over Heorot as a form of revenge stemming from this envy.

Revenge

Revenge serves as a motivating factor for several characters throughout the poem, initially stirring Grendel and his mother. Grendel seeks revenge upon mankind for the heritage that he has been dealt. He delights in raiding Heorot because it is the symbol of everything that he detests about men: their success, joy, glory, and favor in the eyes of God. Grendel's mother's revenge is more specific. She attacks Heorot because someone there killed her son. Although she is smaller and less powerful than Grendel, she is motivated by a mother's fury. When

Beowulf goes after her in the mere, she has the added advantage of fighting him in her own territory. As she drags him into her cave beneath the lake, her revenge peaks because this is the very man who killed her son. Only Beowulf's amazing abilities as a warrior and the intervention of God or magic can defeat her.

Revenge also motivates the many feuds that the poet refers to and is a way of life—and death—for the Germanic tribes. Old enmities die hard and often disrupt attempts at peace, as the poet recognizes. Upon his return to Geatland, Beowulf (2020 ff.) speculates about a feud between Hrothgar's Scyldings and the Heathobards, a tribe in southern Denmark with whom Hrothgar *hopes* to make peace through the marriage of his daughter. Beowulf is skeptical, envisioning a renewal of hostilities. In fact, the Heathobards do later burn Heorot in events not covered by the poem but probably familiar to its audience. Another example of revenge overcoming peace occurs in the Finnsburh section (1068–1159).

Beowulf's final battle is the result of vengeance. A dangerous fire-dragon seeks revenge because a fugitive slave has stolen a valuable cup from the monster's treasure-hoard. His raids across the countryside include the burning of Beowulf's home. Beowulf then seeks his own revenge by going after the dragon.

Major Symbols

A literary symbol is something, often an object, that stands for a significant concept or series of ideas. Often a symbol is emblematic of the values of the characters. In Beowulf, some of the most important symbols are Hrothgar's mead-hall, Grendel's cave, Grendel's arm and head, and the dragon's treasure-trove.

Heorot

Hrothgar's great mead-hall, Heorot ("Hall of the Hart"), functions as both setting and symbol in the epic. It is much more than a place to drink. Symbolically, Heorot represents the achievements of the Scyldings, specifically Hrothgar, and their level of civilization. The hall is a home for the warriors who sleep there and functions as a seat of government. It is a place of light, warmth, and joy, contrasting with Grendel's morbid swamp as well as the dark and cold of winters in Scandinavia. In Heorot, Hrothgar celebrates his victories and rewards his thanes (warriors) with various treasures. The building is like a palace. It towers high and is compared to a cliff. The gables are shaped like horns of the hart. People from neighboring tribes have respectfully contributed to the rich decorations and intricate designs. The hall is also symbolic in that it is the setting of Beowulf's first great battle, the defeat of Grendel. When Grendel invades the hall, he knows that he strikes at the very heart of the Scyldings. That lends special meaning to his victories and to Beowulf's eventual liberation of the hall from the ravages of the ogres.

The Cave

The cave where Grendel and his mother hide from the world is symbolic of their lives as outcasts. Hidden beneath a treacherous mere in the middle of a dark, forbidding swamp, the cave allows them a degree of safety and privacy in a world that they view as hostile. They certainly are not welcome at Heorot, and they know it.

The cave also represents their heritage. As descendants of Cain, they are associated with sorcery, black magic, demons, ancient runes, and hell itself. When Grendel's mother is able to fight Beowulf in the cave, she has a distinct advantage; his victory is all the more significant. It is not clear whether he wins because of his own ability, the influence of magic (the giant sword), or God's intervention. All are mentioned, probably because the poet borrowed from various influences in creating the poem. The cave itself represents a world alien to Heorot. One is high and bright and full of song and joy, towering as the Scyldings' greatest achievement. The other is dark and dank and full of evil, beneath a mere in the middle of a fen and the symbolic home of resentful outcasts.

Grendel's Claw and Head

Beowulf had hoped to have an entire Grendel body to present to King Hrothgar after his battle with the ogre in Heorot. He has to settle for the right arm or claw, ripped from its shoulder socket, when the mortally wounded adversary flees to the swamp. The claw is hung high beneath Heorot's roof (most likely on the outside beneath the gables) as a symbol of Beowulf's victory.

Grendel's mother also sees it as a symbol, representing her personal loss and mankind's macabre sense of what might be an appropriate trophy. Filled with grief and rage, she retrieves the arm from Heorot and kills another Scylding in the process. When Beowulf tracks her to the mere and ends up in her underwater cave, he has no more interest in the claw. Grendel's head, which he is able to find after a strange, perhaps holy brilliance illuminates the dimly lighted cave, is much more impressive. He ignores the vast treasure in the cave, instead choosing to carry the magnificent, huge head as symbolic of his victory over both ogres.

The Dragon's Treasure-Trove

The dragon's treasure-trove poignantly represents the vanity of human wishes as well as the mutability of time. The dragon's barrow holds wealth in abundance, yet the wealth is of no use to anyone. The ancient treasures in the hoard once belonged to a regional tribe of warriors who were killed in battle some 300 years previously. Only one survivor, who is called the "keeper of the rings" (2244), lived to hide the treasures in the barrow.

Just as the dead warriors cannot use the treasure, neither can the dragon. He devotes his life to guarding a treasure that he frankly has no use for. Beowulf gives his life defeating the dragon and gaining this impressive treasure for his people, but they won't benefit from it either. The treasure is buried with the great warrior in his funeral barrow and, we are told, remains there still, a mighty horde of riches that is of absolutely no use to anybody.

CliffsNotes Review

Use this CliffsNotes Review to test your understanding of the original text and reinforce what you've learned in this book. After you work through the review and essay questions, identify the quote section, and the fun and useful practice projects, you're well on your way to understanding a comprehensive and meaningful interpretation of *Beowulf*.

Q&A

1. The mythological character who founded Hrothgar's kingdom was named
   _____.

2. At the first banquet, Unferth taunts Beowulf about a swimming match
   with _____.

3. Hrothgar's great mead-hall is called _____.

4. Beowulf defeats Grendel by ripping off Grendel's _____
   _____.

5. Grendel's mother lives in a cave beneath a dark _____.

6. Beowulf defeats Grendel's mother through the use of a giant
   _____.

7. It takes four men to carry Grendel's _____ back to Heorot.

8. We are told that Beowulf ruled the Geats well for _____ years.

9. The fiery dragon is angry because a fugitive slave stole a valuable
   _____.

10. _____ comes to Beowulf's assistance in the dragon fight and is the
    future Geat king.

Answers: (1) Scyld Scefing (2) Breca (3) Heorot (4) claw or arm at the shoulder (5) mere or lake (6) magic sword (7) head (8) 50 (9) cup or flagon (10) Wiglaf

Identify the Quote: Find Each Quote In *Beowulf*

1. I'll tell you a truth, son of Ecglaf: / never would Grendel have done so much harm, / the awesome monster, against your own leader, / shameful in Heorot, if heart and intention, / your great battle-spirit, were sharp as your words.

2. No poorer I hold my strength in a fight, / my work in battle, than Grendel does his; / and so I will not kill him by a sword, / shear off his life, though I easily might.

3. Turn not to pride, O brave champion! / Your fame lives now, in one strong time. / Soon in their turn sickness or war / will break your strength, or the grip of fire, / overwhelming wave, or sword's swing, / a thrown spear, or hateful old age. . . .

4. . . . the son of Healfdene / gave me [treasures] at my own choice, / which I wish, great king, to bring to you, / to show my good will.

5. I recall the time, when taking the mead / in the great hall, we promised our chief / who gave us these rings, these very armlets, / that we would repay him for these war-helmets, / tempered edges, if he ever needed us.

Answers: (1) [Beowulf's verbal response to Unferth's insult at the first banquet establishes the visitor's self-control and noble spirit.] (2) [Prior to the Grendel fight, Beowulf eschews use of weapons, demonstrating sportsmanship and a desire for even greater reputation.] (3) [Hrothgar's sermon following Beowulf's defeat of Grendel's mother is directed toward the young Geat champion and sets the tone for the remainder of the poem.] (4) [Following the code of the *comitatus*, Beowulf offers his king, Hygelac, the rewards that the Scyldings gave Beowulf.] (5) [Wiglaf berates the other retainers for abandoning their king while Beowulf is struggling with the dragon.]

Essay Questions

1. Discuss the significance of the heroic code of *comitatus* in *Beowulf*, considering specifically the actions of Beowulf as a young warrior, Wiglaf as a young warrior, and the cowardly retainers at the dragon fight.

2. Consider two of the following as symbols: Heorot, Grendel's claw, the cave, or the dragon's treasure-hoard.

3. How does the poet use the theme of revenge in the poem? Consider the motivation of characters such as Grendel, Grendel's mother, and the dragon, as well as Beowulf.

4. Other than Beowulf, who is your favorite character in the poem? Why?

5. What is the importance of Hrothgar's sermon? Cite at least two specific points that he makes and how they affect our understanding of Beowulf.

Practice Projects

1. If you could change anything about *Beowulf*, what would it be? In what way would you change it?

2. Read John Gardner's novel *Grendel* and compare the title character, his mother, or the dragon to their counterparts in the poem.

3. Identify who *your* mythic heroes are. Are they male or female? Do they come from sports? Movies? Cartoons? Folk legends? Some other source? What do you admire about them?

4. As a class project, divide into small groups and present, in the oral tradition, a performance that tells the story of some current or recent event in the school or community. You may use contemporary poetic forms or invent your own. Music might be part of the presentation.

5. In modern English, create ten of your own kennings that refer to people, places, objects, or events in your daily life.

6. Working together, have the class design its own Web site for the epic and decide what will be featured on the various pages.

CliffsNotes Resource Center

The learning doesn't need to stop here. CliffsNotes Resource Center shows you the best of the best—links to the best information in print and online about the author and/or related works. And don't think that this is all we've prepared for you; we've put all kinds of pertinent information at www.cliffsnotes.com. Look for all the terrific resources at your favorite bookstore or local library and on the Internet. When you're online, make your first stop www.cliffsnotes.com where you'll find more incredibly useful information about *Beowulf.*

Books

This CliffsNotes book provides a meaningful interpretation of *Beowulf,* published by Wiley Publishing, Inc. If you are looking for information about related works, check out these other publications:

Bloom's Reviews: Beowulf, edited by Harold Bloom. Under the supervision of the distinguished critic and professor at Yale University, this introductory volume features selections from the critical views of scholars ranging from Henry Wadsworth Longfellow (1845) to James W. Earl (1994), with a brief essay on the *Beowulf* poet and text, a thematic analysis, and an introduction by the editor. Broomall, PA: Chelsea House, 1999.

Beowulf: An Introduction to the Study of the Poem, 3rd ed., by R. W. Chambers. A classic study of the poem and its background. If available, the second edition (1932) features some interesting plates. Cambridge: Cambridge University Press, 1959.

Beowulf: A Dual-Language Edition, edited by Howell D. Chickering, Jr. With facing-page text of the Anglo-Saxon, the translation is modern and captivating while remaining faithful to the original. The editor provides a superior introduction and detailed commentary. If a student were limited to just one book for the study of *Beowulf,* this would be an excellent choice. Highly recommended. New York: Anchor Books, 1977.

Beowulf, by George Clark. For students assigned research papers, the annotated bibliography is a good place to start. Strengths of the text include background and traditions. A chronology of characters and events in the poem is speculative but of some interest. Boston: Twayne publishers, 1990.

Thinking about Beowulf, by James W. Earl. Earl's fresh approach to psychoanalytical "excursions" is worthwhile, and we seldom see a book with *two* introductions by the same author. Stanford: Stanford University Press, 1994.

Grendel, by John Gardner. This touching, humorous, insightful novel tells Grendel's story from the ogre's point of view. Instructors might encourage a comparison of characters and themes in the novel with those in the epic. Highly recommended. New York: Knopf, 1971.

***The Cultural World in* Beowulf,** by John M. Hill. While some beginning students may profit from this detailed study, it probably will benefit advanced scholars more. Detailed endnotes are especially interesting. Toronto: University of Toronto Press, 1995.

The Beowulf Poet: A Collection of Critical Essays, edited by Donald K. Fry. A small but helpful book featuring Tolkien's seminal 1936 essay, Magoun's 1953 article on the oral-formulaic theory, and an introduction by Englewood Cliffs, NJ: Prentice-Hall, 1968.

Interpretations of Beowulf: A Critical Anthology, edited by R. D. Fulk. In addition to works by Tolkien and Magoun, the volume contains several important essays on such diverse topics as irony, tradition, and Christian perspective. Bloomington: Indiana University Press, 1991.

An Anthology of Beowulf Criticism, edited by Lewis E. Nicholson. Many of the early classic essays are here, including Tolkien, Magoun, Rogers' article on the poem's three great fights, Baum's piece on the poet, and several considerations of Christian aspects of the epic. Notre Dame, IN: Notre Dame Press, 1963.

It's easy to find books published by Wiley Publishing, Inc. You'll find them in your favorite bookstores (on the Internet and at a store near you). We also have three Web sites that you can use to read about all the books we publish:

- www.cliffsnotes.com
- www.dummies.com
- www.wiley.com

Internet

Check out these Web resources for more information about *Beowulf:*

The Adventures of Beowulf, http://www.lone-star.net/literature/beowulf/index.html—A serialized adaptation from the Anglo-Saxon with emphasis on episodes; brief introduction.

Anglo-Saxon England: A Guide to Online Resources, http://orb.rhodes.edu/encyclop/early/pre1000/ASindex.html—Offers a series of resources regarding teaching guides, on-line teaching, maps, art works, and related Web sites.

Beowulf Live Recitation Chat, http://www.mobydicks.com/lecture/Beowulfhall/live/chat.cgi—Western Canon University lecture halls and live recitations feature a number of topics of interest to the Beowulf student.

BEOWULF & OLDE ENGLISH Live Chat, http://federalistnavy.com/poetry/BEOWULF&OLDEhall/live/chat.cgi—Part of the Western Canon University classical poets' lecture and chat series.

Beowulf Resources, http://www.georgetown.edu/irvinemj/english016/beowulf/beowulf.html—Features bibliography, consideration of manuscript, and discussion of Old English.

Bulfinch's Mythology, The Age of Fable: Beowulf, http://www.webcom.com/shownet/medea/bulfinch/bul42.html—A detailed consideration of the epic, with suggestions for further browsing and searching.

Electronic Beowulf: A Guide, http://www.uky.edu/%7Ekiernan/eBeowulf/content.html—This is an online guide for the Electronic Beowulf, a set of two CD-ROMs published by British Library Publications and the University of Michigan Press, an image-based edition.

Next time you're on the Internet, don't forget to drop by www.cliffsnotes.com. We created an online Resource Center that you can use today, tomorrow, and beyond.

Articles

Following are articles that can help you understand Beowulf:

Desmond, Marilynn. "*Beowulf:* The Monsters and the Tradition." *Oral Tradition* 7 (1992): 258–83. An update and extension of the background scholarship. Students interested in Grendel and his mother should find this especially rewarding.

Bloomfield, Joan. "The Style and Structure of *Beowulf*." *Review of English Studies* 14 (1938): 396–403. This early study is a good place to start for students interested in the narrative style of the epic.

Send Us Your Favorite Tips

In your quest for knowledge, have you ever experienced that sublime moment when you figure out a trick that saves time or trouble? Perhaps you realized you were taking ten steps to accomplish something that could have taken two. Or you found a little-known workaround that achieved great results. If you've discovered a useful tip that helped you understand Beowulf more effectively and you'd like to share it, the CliffsNotes staff would love to hear from you. Go to our Web site at www.cliffsnotes.com and click the Talk to Us button. If we select your tip, we may publish it as part of CliffsNotes Daily, our exciting, free e-mail newsletter. To find out more or to subscribe to a newsletter, go to www.cliffsnotes.com on the Web.

Index

NOTES

CliffsNotes

LITERATURE NOTES